GARDEN COLOUR SERIES

GARDEN PLANNING AND DESIGN

P Francis Hunt

AURA
EDITIONS

Opposite title page *Basic building materials can be incorporated into a design to give it shape and interest. Here, the combination of different bricks, stones and woods provide the framework for a garden of timeless charm.*
Right *An unusual and imaginative feature of this garden is the positioning of a formal statue beside a self-seeded angelica* (Angelica archangelica) *and its semi-wild surrounds.*

Series Editor: Susan Conder
Editor: Eluned James
Art Editor: Caroline Dewing

Published by
Aura Editions
2 Derby Road
Greenford, Middlesex

Produced by Marshall Cavendish Books Ltd
58 Old Compton Street
London W1V 5PA

© Marshall Cavendish Limited 1985

ISBN 0 86307 274 7

Typeset in Ehrhardt 453 by Walkergate Press, Anlaby
Printed and bound in Hong Kong by Dai Nippon Printing Company

CONTENTS

INTRODUCTION

Whether starting from scratch or working on an existing layout, you can lift your garden out of the ordinary by using the simple secrets of landscape design.

In the past, gardens were planned either for show and pleasure or for vegetable, fruit and flower production. Today, although there are small gardens designed solely for pleasure and others used for food, most are planned to provide crops and enjoyment combined.

The particular form of a garden you want to make depends primarily on its function but another consideration will be the current use of the site and the plants already growing there (unless, of course, it is a fresh plot). Soil type, local climate, and the money you have available must be considered, too.

You must also realize that the garden needs of a family or a single person change greatly over the years and, therefore, the garden must be easily adaptable. A young couple may be quite happy with a mainly grassed and partly shaded area, where lazing in deckchairs is the main activity, enlivened by the occasional barbecue. Babies require a quiet, shaded area for a pram or play-pen in summer, young children a place for tricycles or a sand-pit or swing, and older children a place for ball games. The state of family finances when the children are around could mean that a supply of home-grown fruit and vegetables would be very welcome.

When the children have left home, there will be about twenty years of active gardening ahead of the average gardener, with time, energy and money at their optimum balance. However, retirement usually brings with it a decreased income and a greater intolerance of the extremes of weather. The routine chores of weekly gardening maintenance and the large seasonal tasks can become a burden. A free-standing greenhouse or a lean-to conservatory could then provide pleasure throughout the year, irrespective of the weather, as well as small quantities of fruit and vegetables.

Consider, too, what you want your garden to look like. What is the effect you are trying to achieve? A garden should always be thought of in the context of your own home and the nearby buildings – its style should be in sympathy with its location. Contrasting styles of house and garden can be very successful but it is often better to avoid this.

If you have a thatched country cottage, the 'cottage garden' style is the obvious choice; likewise a 'modern' house of the 1930s suggests bold plants arranged geometrically, and a terraced town-house with a minute backyard is ideal for a paved patio with container-grown shrubs. However, modern estate homes are built in such a diversity of architectural styles and with such a wide range of construction materials that it is often difficult to decide on a style for the oddly-shaped patches of builders' rubble that is often provided as a garden.

Fortunately, there are many other factors which can help to decide style, in particular the idea that the garden is an extension of the home. The internal layout of a house and its interior decor can influence a garden layout and the type of plants to be used.

To most people, however, the immediately relevant factor is the cost of creating a garden. Remember that money is needed not only for the initial construction, but also for the continuing maintenance. In the long term, it is cheaper to spend more on building and stocking a relatively expensive but labour-saving garden now, than to build it too cheaply with low quality materials that require expensive maintenance or replacement after a few years.

In order to reduce costs, many plants can be obtained free from neighbours and usually these plants are better adapted to local conditions than commercial nursery stock. In addition, many of the more expensive, rarer trees and shrubs are now available as seed from specialist seed merchants. These seeds may be more difficult to germinate than well-known garden annuals or vegetables but, once transplanted, are much more likely to become established. In any case, they can be planted closely together and then thinned to allow the best specimens to grow.

Materials for paving, walls, fences and such garden features as seats, greenhouses, sheds, ponds and arches must be of good quality and can be particularly expensive. However, some of the most suitable material is sold secondhand and at low cost.

Probably the greatest satisfaction can be gained by designing and building a garden for your own specific needs from scratch. For some people, however, the ultimate achievement is to enhance and develop an already exisiting garden, particularly if it is overgrown and long untended.

Opposite *A rose garden of traditional design combines simple but effective elements: geometrically arranged beds, rustic trelliswork and neatly trimmed lawns. Even on a much smaller scale, such a design would retain all of its classic elegance.*

CHAPTER 1
ASSESSING YOUR SITE

Before planning your garden in detail, you should assess the site as carefully as possible. Look at its shape and size, find out about its soil and climatic conditions and decide what your main requirements will be for the immediate future.

When you have more or less decided on the kind of garden you would like to have, you should then think about the advantages and disadvantages of the site. If you have the time and money, it is possible to clear the site and create your ideal garden from scratch. Unfortunately, few of us have the patience to do this and, in any case, there may be certain features already existing that really should be saved. Even if they are not wonderful, they could be refurbished to give shelter or screening until more suitable structures can be built and any new plants have established themselves. So, all features of the site should be investigated before constructing or planting anything. Size, shape, soil, climate, access and circulation should be assessed as well as the type and condition of the trees and shrubs already planted.

Shapes and sizes of garden
Gardening books and magazines usually assume that small gardens are either rectangular or square but the truth is often quite different. The size of 'small gardens' can vary from a paved patio 36 sq m (100 sq ft) to a 0.2 hectare (½ acre) plot. Even greater variation is found in the shapes of small gardens. Many are rectangular or square, others are almost linear, and some taper away in various directions. Newer houses, particularly in high-density housing estates, may have very irregularly-shaped plots. They are quite literally the spaces left over after the houses have been built. In some extreme cases, the garden may not even adjoin the home to which it belongs! Nevertheless, do not be disheartened by an oddly-shaped plot, as every space, no matter how unpromising it might seem, has the potential to become your ideal garden.

Aspect
In all gardens, the exposure and general aspects are very important in determining the type of plants to grow and their position. The site may be exposed to all weathers, to the gaze of all the neighbours and to the pedestrians in the adjoining streets. On the other hand, it could be surrounded by the blank wall of office blocks and street walls which, although protecting it from view, also seriously reduces the sunlight and the rainfall.

You should always remember that just as you can look out of your garden, others can look in and you must decide whether you want privacy at all costs or if you wish strangers to admire your handiwork. The distant view, too, may influence your final design. Is it of the open countryside or, say, the local gas works? Another very relevant factor is the view from indoors: most people spend much more time looking at the garden from the kitchen window than from the sitting room and the view from any upstairs rooms will add yet another dimension that you might want to consider.

Climate and microclimates
If the area is generally cold and wet, the vegetable patch should be close to the house to enable you to harvest crops in the wettest weather without getting too soaked and cold. In warmer areas, a shady patio through which cool breezes can flow is a useful feature. These are only two examples of the importance of climate in garden design. Although the overall climate of the area in which you live controls the plants that can and cannot be grown, the success of individual varieties and the flowering and fruiting times of particular specimens depends on the microclimate of the garden itself and of its different parts. Every garden has its own microclimate and, each time a plant is grown or removed, or a wall or other feature is built or demolished, the microclimate is altered.

In any garden both the local and the specific climate must be considered. Temperature, rainfall, duration of direct sunlight, the date of the last spring frost and the first autumn frost, the general direction of the prevailing winds and their speed all determine the form and content of a garden. Late frosts in spring can vary very much from one garden to another and are very important in controlling the time when you can transplant half-hardy or tender

Opposite The climate, soil and general location of a garden are all important factors in its design. Very few sites are perfectly level, for example, and most have awkward shapes or shady corners that will need careful planning.

plants. Late frosts can be a crucial factor affecting the pollination of fruit trees. Gardens in a hollow are particularly vulnerable to frost because cold air sinks and accumulates in low-lying pockets. Such gardens can be up to three weeks 'late' compared with those in adjoining areas.

Town gardens and pollution

The presence of cities, large towns and industrial areas can affect gardens in several ways. The large amount of heat generated by machines and office blocks alters the local climate by raising the average temperatures by up to 3°C (5°F) and can even make a garden virtually frost-free. The tallest buildings can intercept rain-bearing clouds and create a rain- Of particular concern is the atmospheric pollution given off by some factories. It has been thought that very dilute pollution can actually be beneficial to some plants by controlling pests and diseases but, in other cases, the pollution is so concentrated that even when crops will grow they should not be eaten and many flowers never come into full bloom. Even if the pollution has no visible effect on the plants themselves, the soil micro-organisms can be affected and

Below *The city environment has influenced the design of this garden and the kind of plants that are growing in it. Shrubs and climbers help to screen off the surrounding buildings, while an old fig tree (Ficus carica) flourishes in the sheltered conditions.*

Below right *In this basement garden, the main consideration is privacy and almost every available space around the sitting-out area has been crowded with lush foliage and colourful pot plants.*

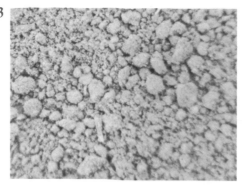

Left The texture of a soil is determined by the size of the particles in it and is critical because it affects the amount of air and water that reaches the plant roots. Clay soils are mostly made up of very fine particles which swell when they are wet and quickly block air from the roots. By adding plenty of organic material, clay can be made into a fertile and easily worked medium. Sandy soil, by contrast, comprises large, gritty particles through which water drains quickly and carries away essential nutrients. The addition of organic material and regular watering will greatly improve it.

1 Loamy sand
2 Clay
3 A well-balanced loam
4 A sandy clay loam

Below A little effort and some imagination could transform this lacklustre site into a colourful and well-designed garden.

this can reduce the fertility of the soil.

Dust and soot, although not poisonous, can clog the breathing pores of plants and stunt their growth. Salt is quite commonly found in the air up to 8 km (5 miles) from the coast and can damage many plants. It is much better to go and see what grows well in parks and gardens along the coast and use the same sort of plants than to try to grow your favourites only to have them die or become increasingly stunted. Many of the seaside plants grow even better inland!

Your garden's soil

A well-known broadcaster on gardening topics used to reply to a great number of questions that the answer lay in the soil. Soils are very important in the life of plants. Apart from a few, true rock-dwellers and floating water-plants, all plants require soil to provide most of their food and water and to give them anchorage. The most important aspects of a soil are its depth, physical nature and chemical composition. Before a successful garden can be created it is essential to find out as much as possible about the soil. Not only does this tell you which plants to grow, it also indicates the treatment that may be necessary to improve or even to alter conditions so that you can grow a greater variety of plants.

A soil is not a uniform covering of small stones, sand and clay spread evenly over the earth's surface. It varies from place to place and, even in a small garden, can be different in every part of the plot. All soils contain sand and clay and are classified according to which is dominant. By adding organic matter (humus), clay or sand soils can be greatly improved. The best soil has a near-perfect combination of these three basic ingredients and is known as loam. Soils develop very slowly from the weathered base rock acted upon by the climate, the vegetation cover and man's activities over hundreds of years. Being arranged in layers, soils also vary from top to bottom The vital layer for plants is the topsoil. This can be as shallow as 7.5cm (3in) or as deep as 6m (20ft) but most gardens have about 30cm (1ft) overlying the subsoil. In turn, there

A derelict garden before and after renovation. By following the original layout fairly closely, the feeling of old-fashioned charm has been retained although the immediate impression is very different.

can be a varying depth of subsoil on top of the base rock. Some gardens on new sites have no topsoil at all or have a covering of builders' rubble. In other gardens the subsoil may have been brought to the surface. In these cases it is probably easier to buy a load of good topsoil from a nurseryman or alternatively from a landscape contractor.

Digging by hand is still the best way to improve a soil. It aerates the soil, improves the drainage, kills the smaller weeds, allows you to remove the larger weeds and incorporates manure and other organic material into the soil structure. In neglected or new garden sites, a major problem can be severely compacted soil devoid of many of the micro-organisms essential for fertility. A mechanical cultivator can be used in these cases but the final stages before planting should be done by hand, using a spade or fork. There can never be too much organic matter dug into a soil and although rotted stable manure and straw are the best, almost any waste household or plant material can be used. There are many proprietary brands of soil conditioner which can be successful but they are very expensive when compared with free waste materials.

Many plants are very sensitive to the degree of acidity or alkalinity of the soil. Rhododendrons, for example, are best grown on acid soils while scabious (*Scabiosa* spp.) prefer alkaline soils. The soil acidity or alkalinity is usually quoted as a pH number, with pH 7 being neutral (above 7 is alkaline and below 7 is acid). The pH of any soil can be easily measured, using simple kits obtainable from garden centres and nurserymen. Most of these kits are very useful for giving not only the pH figure but also details of what should be done to the soil to alter its acidity or alkalinity.

The speed at which water drains through the soil and the amount which is retained in it has a great effect on plant growth. By and large, sandy soils are very well-drained and retain very little water whereas clay soils drain slowly and can easily become very heavy and waterlogged. Fortunately, most garden soils contain both sand and clay and, therefore drainage or water retention is not a major problem. However, nearly all soils require some watering in a dry season, particularly when plant growth is at its peak in the warmest months.

Water drainage and 'run-off' on the surface are also controlled by the slope of the garden. These gradients in a garden are not always obvious but a survey of the levels can be carried out quite easily and is usually very worthwhile.

Existing plants

Most garden plots have some existing vegetation even if it is only a few weeds or neglected trees and shrubs. It is important to note all the plants before deciding to remove any. Some may be mature and, healthy and could well remain where they are growing in the new plan. Some may be younger specimens that would transplant easily to a more useful spot and others, although not wanted in the long term, could still be useful to give protection to new plants you want to add. It is better to retain a cover of weeds to stabilize the soil on a slope than to remove it before you are really ready to plant. A knowledge of the plants on a garden site, useful or not, gives an indication of the type of plant that does well there and certainly will show up those that are not really at home.

Even old shrubs and trees can often be rejuvenated by cutting them down to encourage new growth from the base. Apart from 'weed' trees such as many elms and sycamores, all trees should be checked to see if they are healthy. Those that have many dead or weak branches may have to be removed but, by careful pruning and, perhaps, bracing of the larger limbs, many fine old specimens can be saved. It is usually better and certainly safer to employ a professional tree surgeon to undertake this sort of work, than to attempt to undertake it yourself.

When a tree has to be cut down there often remains an old tree trunk in the ground. It can be rotted away slowly by chemicals but it is quicker to have it removed by a contractor or tree surgeon. However, considerable expense can be spared by keeping it as a base for a garden seat or table or letting clematis, ivies or other climbers cover it.

If you decide to move some plants to another spot, it is better to do this in late autumn, late winter or early spring. Conifers and other evergreens should always be transplanted in the spring. It is possible to move plants at other times, but the losses can be great and, in the hotter days of summer, it is essential that all transplants are copiously watered for several weeks afterwards.

Access and circulation

Many garden plans seem ideal until the time comes to mow the grass, show an elderly or disabled person around, or take delivery of a do-it-yourself greenhouse or garden shed. You could then discover that it is very difficult to manhandle a heavy lawnmower over a flower-bed or across a rock garden, that the wheelchair carrying an invalid will not fit the paths, or that the garden gate is not big enough to pass the pieces of garden shed through.

Access to a garden and circulation within it must always be given top priority. Garden plans should begin with an indication of the routes to, from and in the garden. The paths to everyday features such as the dustbin, the compost heap and the bicycle shed or greenhouse should be direct and as short as possible. They should also be wide enough to take a wheel-barrow, a pram or a wheelchair and, ideally, two people should be able to walk side by side.

Curving paths may seem ideal on a plan but they can lead to 'unofficial' tracks being made across the edge of a lawn or flower-bed in order to reach somewhere quicker.

Garden steps and terraces should always be accompanied by a gently sloping ramp both for wheeled vehicles and for the elderly, the very young and the infirm, all of whom may find steps difficult.

There must always be at least one entrance to a garden that is wide enough to accommodate large plants, pieces of garden furniture and awkwardly-shaped machinery. This is important even if the only entrance is through the house.

Above *A problem like the stump of a dead tree can be turned to advantage by letting fast-growing climbers, such as ivy, transform it into a decorative feature.*

Left *Bricks are easy to lay for making curved paths in an informal garden. Here, they skirt a bed at the foot of a tree and, to soften the lines still further, self-seeded plants and tufts of grass have been allowed to grow between the bricks.*

CHAPTER 2
DESIGNING & DRAWING UP YOUR PLAN

Once you have measured your site and noted the position of any permanent features such as good or bad views, you can begin to sketch in the elements of its overall design and decide how much space to allocate to each one.

Before any measuring or drawing-up of a detailed garden plan is to be done, you should sit down and design the garden in your mind's eye. A very rough plan of the site can be useful at this stage, just to remind you of the site's limitations (caused perhaps by neighbouring houses and the street outside), and of the opportunities offered by good existing plants and, perhaps, views to the distant countryside. It is always useful to discuss your plans with your family, your neighbours and your friends but in the end only you can really decide what you want and what can reasonably be achieved.

Sit down in various parts of the garden, stand by the garden gate or the kitchen, lounge or bedroom window and visualize what you would like to see. Do not limit your imagination to what you would like in midsummer when all the flowers are in full bloom, or to mid-autumn when the trees and shrubs are just shedding their red, yellow and brown leaves, or to spring when the earliest daffodils, crocuses and snowdrops are just peeping through. Think about your garden at less attractive times of the year. It is easy to imagine it in midwinter, when snow has covered all its imperfections, but what about late autumn when the first really heavy frosts have blackened the leaves of high-summer plants, or late summer when the grass has turned brown? Try to imagine it as a place to be enjoyed at all times: do you really want unwieldy large trees, masses of tender summer plants or big patches of easily scorched lawns?

Take a stroll into the street outside or even ask your neighbours if you can look at your property from the vantage points in their gardens, so that you can see your ideal garden as others will eventually see it.

The purpose of a garden
Day-dreaming at this stage should be counteracted, or at least balanced, by practicalities. Keep in your mind that a garden has four main uses. Firstly, it must set off your house to its best advantage, camouflaging the ugly bits and emphasizing the best aspects. Ideally, you should consider the house and garden as equal partners occupying your site.

Secondly, a garden is for flowers and ornamental plants to be enjoyed at all seasons and from all angles. Thirdly, it is a place in which to relax, entertain or play and, finally, it can be a source of food. These last three uses need not be of the same importance nor occupy equal spaces, but can be catered for according to your priorities.

The vegetable and fruit garden
Small gardens may only have enough space for growing a few plants of thyme, chives and parsley in a window box. It may be practicable in slightly larger plots to grow some vegetables among the flowers. Sweet corn, runner beans and red cabbages can be grown among the decorative plants in a mixed border. There are now many edible beets and cabbages with multi-coloured leaves grown purely for display as well as the attractive tree onion (*Allium cepa* 'Prolifera') or the globe artichoke.

The growing of vegetables in any case should not be thought of as a means of saving a lot of money. The vegetables in shops, stalls and supermarkets are usually grown on specialized farms and market gardens in which large scale operations mean that they can be produced at less cost than in your garden. Paradoxically, the centralized marketing system for commercially grown crops means that they are usually cheaper in cities than in the countryside. Vegetables and fruit should be included in the plans for a small garden for the convenience of having really fresh food easily available, particularly salad crops, which deteriorate quickly.

Some idea of the space needed for

Opposite *Once your ideas have taken shape and you have a clear picture of the kind of garden you think you would like, try drawing up a detailed plan of the design.*

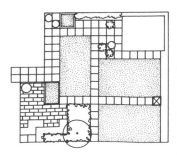

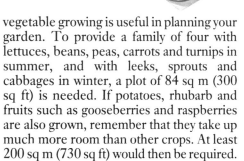

Even on a small site, careful planning will make it possible to be relatively self-sufficient. Most of this garden is taken up by three vegetable plots, measuring about 2.5 × 4m (7 × 12ft), to allow for the correct rotation of crops. Every spare corner is used, with strawberries in pots, fruit trees against the fencing and a bee hive at the end of the path. Next to the house is a small terrace with a herb bed beyond, while the other corner makes a utility area for the compost and rubbish bins.

vegetable growing is useful in planning your garden. To provide a family of four with lettuces, beans, peas, carrots and turnips in summer, and with leeks, sprouts and cabbages in winter, a plot of 84 sq m (300 sq ft) is needed. If potatoes, rhubarb and fruits such as gooseberries and raspberries are also grown, remember that they take up much more room than other crops. At least 200 sq m (730 sq ft) would then be required.

To become fully self-sufficient in vegetables and fruit at least 400 sq m (1500 sq ft) would be needed.

If space is limited, concentrate on 'perpetual' or 'cut-and-come-again' strains of green vegetables, such as broccoli and spinach, or high-yielding plants, such as marrows and dwarf beans, and salad crops such as radishes, lettuces, spring onions and tomatoes.

The sitting-out area

Consider the sitting-out and play area carefully, as it will be the major centre of activity. Ideally, this area should be paved and just outside the kitchen door so that food can easily be passed in and out, vegetables prepared on a warm day and muddy boots removed there in winter. However, if the garden side of the house faces north, you will have to consider a south- or west-facing site further away from the house. This will also need to have a well-drained and mud-free path joining it to the house door.

Depending on where you live and on your own preferences, the sitting-out area can be used to watch the people walking by in the street or nearby park, or the neighbours working in their gardens. Always remember, however, that if you can see out, other people can also see in!

The ornamental garden

The ornamental part of the garden has to be thought of for its total effect, often linking together all the other parts and features. To many gardeners, it will also be a place where favourite plants can be grown as specimens as well as contributing to the overall pattern of plants.

A common mistake is to assume that all gardens must have a mown lawn. Certainly, a well-kept lawn sets off colourful flower-beds and can be used as an extension of the sitting and play areas. But a lawn requires constant attention if it is to continue looking good. There is nothing more distracting in a small garden than an overgrown, weedy lawn, particularly when it is dead-looking at the end of the summer. Ground-cover plants like ivies (*Hedera* species), heathers (*Calluna vulgaris* and *Erica* spp.) and creeping comfrey *(Symphytum grandiflorum)* are less demanding and will thrive in places too uneven or too steep for lawns, although they cannot withstand wear and tear. Stepping stones can be used in these places.

At this stage there is no need to note exactly which varieties of decorative plants are to be used but their places should be roughly decided. Keep in mind their approximate height, spread and rate of growth, and the purpose – or purposes – you want them to fulfill. These could include screening and privacy, shelter from wind, sun and rain, summer flowers, autumn leaf colours or winter fruits and attractive bark colour.

Many ornamental plants, especially larger trees and shrubs, will be grown as specimens by themselves, but the smaller plants will almost certainly be grouped in borders. The width of flower beds and shrub borders needs particular attention: if you make them much over 2m (6ft) wide it could be difficult to handweed or hoe without trampling. If they are too narrow, there will be little room for effective arrangement of plants. Aim for year-round interest: as one plant finishes its display there should be another kind close by to take its place.

Structures in the garden

The siting of individual structures, particularly the less attractive ones, such as dustbins and oil-tanks, can be difficult. It is easier to look after them and hide them from view if they can be grouped. Unfortunately this will often conflict with access: the coal-shed should be close to a good path to the house, the oil-tank needs a clear run for the delivery-man's feed pipe, the dustbin must be close to the garden gate but not too far from the kitchen door. The greenhouse should be in a sunny spot but with some screening in midsummer. If it is a 'lean-to' or conservatory type the house-wall will protect it from frosts but can reflect too much heat in summer. A free-standing, east-to-west greenhouse is probably better.

The front garden

At this early planning stage, hard standing and good access for a boat, caravan or visitors' cars must be considered. This will probably have to be in the front garden, which is very small with most houses. Unfortunately, the front garden is what visitors first see! Ideally, the front garden should be welcoming to guests and provide safe, well-lit and easy access for young and old, fit and disabled, to the front door. It is very much a challenge to combine these with a space for a boat, caravan or car and at the same time not obscure the view from the front room's windows. Privet (*Ligustrum ovalifolium*) and Leyland cypress (×

Above *This storage space for dustbins and fuel is accessible to the street but, because of its covering of ivy and honeysuckle, manages to preserve a garden atmosphere.*

Below *This design for a family with young children includes a grassy play area and sandpit with cycle track around. The pergola hides the front of a garage and provides a shady space for a pram or other toys.*

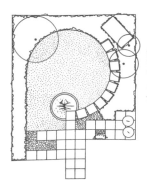

As children get older, a large terraced area will give them room for different activities, while a shed can be used for bicycles, a workshop or playroom. The soft, grassed area can be reduced in size by including a shallow garden pool which will add less functional interest.

Cupressocyparis leylandii) hedges are ideal as thick screens preventing strangers from looking in but they are visually dull and few plants can grow with them because they dry up the soil in summer and cast a deep shade. Other hedging plants you can use are barberries (*Berberis* spp.) roses (*Rosa* spp. and hybrids) and hardy fuchsias (*Fuchsia magellanica* and its varieties) but they are not so easily trimmed and can quickly overhang the paths, especially when dripping wet after a storm. The front part of a garden often needs much more thought than the back, although it is usually smaller.

The practical garden

Whatever pattern of garden finally forms in your mind, remember that your ideal garden must be translated into reality. Not all building materials or plants are readily available in all areas. Paving stones can be prohibitively expensive if they have to be transported a long distance and plants bought from a nursery in one area do not always transplant well in another. Bricks are a very satisfying material for paths as well as walls but, unless they are laid properly, they can be damaged by wear and tear. Professional help may be too expensive and you may not have the expertise or time or even confidence to do it yourself.

You may have decided that a garden pool is essential for your garden. With water plants in summer flower, fish in the clear water and the constantly changing reflection of the sky, a pool is a very attractive proposition. Pools require a lot of attention, though, and during the hottest days of summer you may have to top-up the water level every day. Plants grow quickly in water and you have to keep them under control or they will take over and leave no room for the fish.

Drawing up a plan

The very rough plan you have been using to help your ideas take shape must now be drawn out more accurately so that you can work out precisely the number and kinds of plants and the correct amounts of building materials.

Fortunately, if you live in one of the many newer houses, there is probably a plan of your house plot attached to your title deeds. If not, the local library or council planning department may let you trace your site boundaries from their large-scale maps. Even if this is not possible, it is very easy to draw your own site plan.

First of all you should measure the edges of your site, including the house, whether it occupies just a corner or the whole width. Using squared graph paper and working at a scale of about 1 to 50 (i.e. 2cm on paper equals 1 metre on the ground or ¼in equals 1ft) draw these measurements as lines. With some adjustment the four or more corners will meet! The size and shape of the house should then be added and you should also plot all the existing features that cannot be moved. These include manhole covers, water stop-taps and garden entrances to the house and road. Remember that all the space not occupied by your house is available for your garden. Even if house and garden are very small, they should always be treated together in just the same way as the early landscape architects such as 'Capability' Brown treated country mansions and palaces as part of the surrounding landscape.

Plants that cannot be moved should be plotted, as well as those that you want to move elsewhere or get rid of altogether. As you develop your plan on paper you may well have to rethink some of your earlier decisions. Some favourite plants may have to be abandoned and not-so-good specimens may have to be kept for a while until others have grown up.

Next on your plan you should draw the circulation within the garden and the routes to and from each feature. Straight lines between two points are usually preferred by people in a hurry but are not always pleasing to look at. A gently curving path is usually best but remember that when turned into reality from the plan, the foreshortening of it by the eye can make it almost too winding. A symmetrical and formal plan built around a straight central path with the dustbins at the far end, the sitting-out area next to the house and a flower-garden one side of the path and the vegetable garden on the other may look very neat on paper but is very dull in real life. An informal layout with an off-centre path giving access to all parts is just as easy to build and often much easier to maintain. If it changes slightly from year to year it does not matter but a symmetrical layout will look very odd if only one feature is out of place.

It is useful now to mark out the design on the site itself using sticks, string and stones and ignoring the present garden. You should walk up and down where the paths will be, sit where the play and relaxation area is planned and pretend to work where the vegetables will be grown. It is surprising how many minor re-adjustments or even major rethinking may be required when you have actually seen the plan roughly transferred to the ground.

Eventually, however, you will decide exactly what is possible and desirable and you should then draw up the final design. The paths should now be drawn to scale and the varieties of plants inserted on the plan. Finally you should ink in all the main lines you have drawn as well as the dots marking the positions of plants. Rub out the pencil lines and then have a few copies made on a photocopier. It is very easy for your only plan to blow away and be lost or to perhaps get trodden on by a very muddy boot!

Now you are ready to start to create your garden, remember that it will be many seasons before it is exactly as you visualized. Trees and shrubs take a long time to reach a satisfactory size. However, before planting you can start to build the necessary surrounds, the walls, paths and other structures.

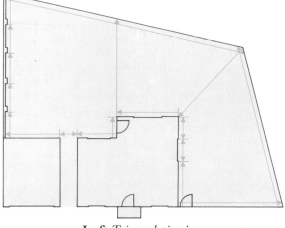

Right *The first step in drawing up an accurate plan of your garden is to mark in the house and any other large buildings such as a garage or greenhouse. Include all ground floor windows and doors so that you can think about access and view points. With this done, mark in the site boundaries: if your site is reasonably regular in shape, you should be able to plot them by extending lines at 90 degrees from the house.*

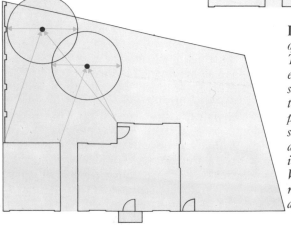

Left *Triangulation is an accurate way of plotting the features in your garden. To pinpoint the position of a tree, for example, measure its distance from two separate places. Use a pair of compasses to draw arcs from these points on your plan: their radii should be reduced to scale and should correspond to the distances measured. The arcs will intersect at the exact location of the tree. When marking it onto your plan, remember to include the overhang area, as this will affect what you can grow.*

CHAPTER 3
GARDEN BUILDING MATERIALS

The variety of building materials available will provide you with a host of design possibilities involving colour, texture and overall shape so take a look at as many examples as you can before making your final choice.

The kind of building materials you can use for making garden features are determined by four main factors: cost, availability, ease of use, and, most important of all, suitability for the job.

Natural materials such as stones, gravel, wood and manufactured types like concrete, bricks and tiles, have now been joined by entirely man-made products such as rigid and flexible plastics. A recent innovation is the use of special materials added to provide great strength and increased durability, an example being glass-reinforced concrete.

Do not overlook the possibilities offered by second-hand materials. These can help the garden to take on a matured and more natural look soon after construction. Old bricks from a demolished house (provided they are suitable for garden use), or disused wooden railway sleepers or telegraph poles, sawn into shorter lengths, are sometimes obtainable from garden centres and builders' merchants. If you do buy any materials, check them carefully for any flaws.

When choosing any materials you must always remember that the cheapest is not necessarily the bargain it may seem. It may be less costly to buy some but the 'special offer' maintenance costs may be much higher, and parts may need replacing more often. In any case, whatever the price, the materials you buy must be suitable for your garden.

Bricks and tiles
One of the most pleasing and useful materials is brick, but it requires considerable care in choice and installation.

Bricks blend well with most plants, and with other building materials, and they are equally appropriate in town, suburban and country gardens, for formal or informal layouts. You can use bricks as a background to plants for the very practical reason that they soak up the sun's heat and release it slowly over a long period. This provides a favourable microclimate for ripening fruit. The more tender trees such as apricots and peaches grow particularly well against brick walls. There is another great advantage with bricks and that is their wide availability in a great choice of colours, textures, sizes and shapes. Yellow, blue, grey, brown, black as well as many shades of traditional red; rough, smooth; dimpled, flaked and ribbed bricks are usually on sale at builders' merchants or, sometimes, at large garden centres. Each part of the country generally has one predominant brick type due to the local clay from which they are made. It is often cheaper to buy these and, of course, they are usually much more in keeping with the character and building style of the area than 'foreign' ones.

You can also use bricks that have already been used once. These can be obtained from demolition contractors and are much cheaper than new ones. Having weathered over a number of years, re-used bricks quickly create a mellow, well-established look in a new garden. Bear in mind, however, that not all bricks used for buildings are equally suitable for paths and garden walls – the more exposed use may cause some of them to flake or crumble.

The cost of bricks is about twice that of concrete blocks but not usually as much as that of natural stones. Bricks, as well as being used for paths, terraces, sitting-out areas, small walls, and as a base for garden buildings, can be used for high walls, though a brick wall over 60cm (24in) high will need to be 'full brick' (double thickness), or have strengthening piers. A wall that is long, or over 1.8m (6ft) high will need ties and considerable re-inforcing even though it is built to double thickness. In such cases, the higher cost of bricks is very noticeable. Moreover, unless you are already a good bricklayer, any brick wall over 1.8m (6ft) should be built under close professional guidance and this again can greatly increase the cost of the wall.

Opposite *Bricks can be particularly useful for building projects in the garden. They are hard wearing and can be laid in many unusual patterns to create different effects.*

Top *Walls can be built in a variety of different patterns, according to the way the bricks are laid. The most common pattern, in which the bricks all have their long faces visible, is needed for single thickness walls. In double thickness walls, more complex and less monotonous patterns can be created by using other types of bonding. You can experiment with these patterns by laying a few courses of dry bricks.*

Above *While the same material for walls, paving and seating will create a unified effect different bonding patterns and the natural differences in brick colour will combine to make a more interesting finish.*

However, lower brick walls can be laid quite easily by any reasonably good do-it-yourself gardener providing it is remembered that a single-thickness wall requires a double thickness re-inforcing pillar about every 3m (10ft). At these points the underlying foundations must be correspondingly stronger.

Bricks are laid in a number of different patterns called 'bonds'. Which one you choose may be influenced partly by its strength or use, and partly on its decorative effect. When you are building a long wall it is a good idea to vary the bond every so often to avoid it looking very monotonous. If the wall has to bear any weight, either on top, as with a shed or greenhouse, or at the side as with a terrace support, the bond must be very strong, but if the wall is not load-bearing you can experiment with different patterns. It may even be un-bonded such as a basket-weave effect, but horizontal reinforcing rods or steel-mesh laid along the mortar joints of such designs is essential.

Double brick walls can be built with a wide space between the two layers that can be packed with soil and plants grown along the top of the walls. However, so that the soil does not become water-logged you should leave a few un-mortared spaces ('weep holes') for drainage. Although not as strong or as private as a solid wall, 'honeycomb' brick walls can be attractive, especially in older gardens. They are very easy to lay, give support for plants and, despite the holes, provide a pleasant and effective windbreak.

Manufactured by a similar process as that for bricks, quarry tiles give an elegant and durable paving surface that is virtually maintenance-free. They can be bought in many colours, sizes and shapes, including the interlocking tiles; these give added strength to well-used areas.

Stone and gravel

Natural materials like stone and gravel can be used in any garden but are usually expensive. It is best to use those that are in common usage in your area; if stones from another area are used they can look very much out of place. In some areas it may even be an offence under the planning regulations to build a boundary wall out of the wrong material. Your local council planning office should be asked for advice before you buy any natural stones for a high boundary wall. If you have just moved to a new area, have a walk around the neighbourhood to see what and how local materials have been used successfully.

It is also very important with natural materials to build with them in the locally acceptable manner. A dry-stone wall may bring back memories of the countryside in your schooldays but in the suburbs of a large city, or in the garden of a terraced house, it may look very much out of place. In the same way, a solid concrete wall in the countryside looks equally odd. Fortunately, locally used stones are generally much cheaper than those from elsewhere.

Natural walls may be of 'hard' or 'soft' stones. Commonly used hard stones include granite and flint, the soft ones are limestones and sandstones. Soft stones are ideal for walls as they are fairly easy to trim and lay as well as forming a sympathetic background to the plants to be grown on and in front of them. Where there will be most wear and tear, granite and other hard stones are more suitable. You can buy hard and soft stones as rough-cut rubble, more or less as it was quarried, as squared rubble which is fairly evenly cut, or ashlar, which is square-shaped with a smooth finish.

Quarry-finished stones are available with a variety of textures and surface patterns.

Rough-cut rubble is always laid in a random fashion but regular blocks and ashlar are laid in 'courses' in the same way as bricks and concrete blocks. Patterns such as the herring-bone 'Cornish Hedge' can be made but stones lose much of their strength if not laid along their natural grain. Not all blocks of stone are the same size and shape unless you are prepared to pay very much more for them.

When you build a wall of mixed blocks considerable care is needed to make sure the finished result is really as strong as it will look. Mortar is generally used between the blocks but in some parts of the country experts build dry walls, which are almost as strong as mortared ones. All stone walls should be built on a good concrete foundation at least 30cm (1ft) deep and always at least twice as wide as the wall. If you have plenty of stone available you can use stone 'footings' instead of concrete foundations. However, with any stone wall over 1m (3ft) high you should take professional advice; in any case, you should always get help when building a stone wall, especially if you are not used to handling and carrying such heavy objects for long periods. Many 'bad backs' and 'slipped discs' are caused by unusual gardening operations!

Natural stone walls can weather quite rapidly if not properly protected by a continuous waterproof coping course laid along the top. It need not be of the same stone as the wall itself. Other natural materials like slates are often used, but bricks, roof-tiles and cast concrete are usually quite acceptable. When concrete is used upright stones can be inserted into it to give a castle-like appearance. Never use broken glass to top a wall.

Gravel is widely used in the building industry and is of two main types, natural

1 *The joints in a dry course wall will gradually fill with soil and stone chips and be ideal for creeping plants.*
2 *Each block in this dry wall has been separately shaped and the gaps between filled in with small chippings.*
3 *Reconstituted stone blocks have variable colours, shapes and textures.*
4 *A dry stone wall of round boulders and flat slabs needs skilfull work.*
5 *A more formal mortared wall has been carefully brushed to give it the appearance of a dry stone construction.*
6 *Mounted on a mortared rubble core, cut and uncut flints look striking.*
7 *This wall is known as a 'Cornish hedge'. Slabs are laid in flat courses and a herringbone pattern.*
8 *If used apart from natural stone, reconstituted types can look convincing and effective.*
9 *A heavily mortared rubble wall is softened by a rambling clematis.*

Borders alongside a gravel path soften its formal lines. Verbascum, fatsia and white-flowering hydrangeas make a composition of cool greens, while an isolated clump of Alchemilla mollis *adds a natural, 'self-seeded' look.*

and processed. Both are quite acceptable for garden uses such as paths, scree beds and other open areas. Traditionally gravel was obtained as small water-worn pebbles from river beds and much of the gravel sold today is of this type dug up from local gravel pits. In many parts of the country truly natural gravel is not available or is very expensive and, therefore, a substitute has to be used. This is generally crushed limestone or granite 'chippings'. It is not rounded, being angular, but it is very cheap to buy and readily available in various sizes or mixed.

Gravels can be used for all paved areas except where there is very heavy use or where the soil of adjoining beds is very wet and sticky. There is one great advantage in using gravel on a path – small plants will grow in it and soften the otherwise hard edges. You should always prevent the gravel from spreading on to the soil by using

kerbing blocks or narrow planks of well-preserved wood secured by small pegs of wood driven into the ground. For a more natural look, unbarked poles can be used for this and are very cheap to install. However, they may need replacing after three or four years.

If you have an awkward corner in your garden, possibly a patch of subsoil clay or builders' rubbish, you could cover it with gravel to give a very attractive feature in which many kinds of plant can be grown. You will need about 5cm (2in) of medium-sized gravel to cover it. This will partly smooth out any irregular mounds and smother most weeds already there. Rock garden plants should be planted in little pockets of soil and then the gravel scattered around their roots. The gravel will also act as a moisture-retaining mulch during the summer. Before long all you will have to do is trim the plants before they start

competing with each other for space.

Quarried granite shaped into cubes or rectangular blocks called 'setts', and large, rounded pebbles called 'cobbles' were once the most widely used road-surface materials in cities and towns. Nowadays asphalt and concrete have taken over but cobbles and setts arc increasingly being used in pedestrian shopping areas and are very useful and exceptionally hard-wearing for garden use. Cobbles and setts can be expensive but small quantities are sometimes available from a local council's roads department. You must remember, however, that it is usually illegal to remove cobbles from beaches, even in small quantities.

Wood

Wood was once a very cheap building material for garden use but, as over 90 per cent of the timber used in this country is now imported, it can be very expensive. However, it is often obtainable second-hand, when it can be very cheap. Even new, it is generally much cheaper than bricks, concrete or stones.

Wood is used for building garden structures like sheds, summerhouses, pergolas, seats and tables, as a screening and fencing material and, occasionally, for paths and steps. Before being used in the garden, all timber should be treated to prolong its life by reducing insect and fungal attack.

You can buy most new timber already treated. It is usually much cheaper to brush or soak it with preservatives yourself, although professional pressure or vacuum impregnation is better. The traditional chemical to use is creosote, but you must be careful not to splash it on to plants or into your eyes as it can be dangerous. Even its fumes can kill nearby plants when newly applied.

There are now proprietary brands of wood preservative available from shops and garden centres that are easier to apply than creosote and more pleasant to work with. Even so, most are based on poisonous copper chemicals and care must still be taken when using them. The great advantage most of them have over creosote is that they come in a variety of colours including cedar, green and even transparent to retain the appearance of the wood underneath.

Old sawn-off telegraph poles or disused railway sleepers are very useful for paths, stepping 'stones' or supports for terraces and banks because they would have been pressure-treated with preservatives when they were uscd the first time. Railway sleepers can be expensive if bought from a garden centre but they are also available from contractors appointed by British Rail.

Top left *Concrete slabs, cobbles and brick make an interesting contrast of colour, form and texture.*

Bottom left *Set around a tree a radiating pattern of cobbles has been fringed with a double row of bricks.*

Below left *Built along the same lines as a wooden fence, this pergola has added an attractive and shady nook to the garden.*

Below *Simple notched joints* (**1**) *can be strengthened with a T-shaped brace* (**2**) *which will help to reduce side sway on the posts. A double beam and spacer block bolted through the posts* (**3**) *will give more interest to a framework that is viewed from above.*
Bottom *Support posts can be fixed in a poured concrete foundation set into the ground.*

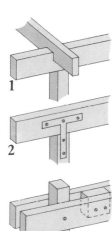

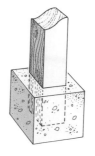

Above *An informal touch has been given to this patio by the inclusion of sawn-off sections of timber that serve as steps, play features and decoration all in one.*

Right *Timber discs can be used as individual stepping stones or, as here, to form a continuous paved surface.*

You cannot, however, buy sleepers direct from British Rail.

It does not matter if the wood you use has already been treated or you have done it yourself, you must always apply a fresh coat of preservative at least once every five years to prevent rot. One of the more expensive timbers is red cedar but it has the exceptional property of being virtually rot-proof. It has a disadvantage in that it is not so strong as timbers like oak and, therefore, cannot be used for wide unsupported spans such as in larger greenhouses, but for smaller structures and as a cladding it is unbeatable. When you consider that it does not need preservatives and rarely needs replacing, it is much cheaper in the long run.

Very thin pieces of wood such as small branches and twigs have been used for centuries as supports for crops like peas and beans and in herbaceous borders. They may not last as long as metal supports and plastic netting but are much cheaper and quickly become covered with plants to give a natural look.

Bamboo canes last longer than twigs, especially if you remember to soak the end in a wood preservative before use. Ideally, you should use a brand of preservative that does not harm plants; if you do use creosote make sure it dries well first. An advantage of canes is that, even when the ends have rotted away, you can still use the middles as shorter canes or split them to make supports for house plants.

Large pieces of timber such as old tree trunks can be used as the base for garden benches and tables. If the trunk is still in the ground, where you have cut down an old tree for example, there is always the chance that it will start to grow again. In this case you must continually prune away all shoots that sprout even if they are several yards away. Incidentally, willow branches nearly always take root when pushed into the ground and many fine willows in suburban gardens today started off as makeshift posts during the Second World War!

Concrete and reconstructed stone

Many people shudder at the thought of using concrete in the garden, except perhaps for foundations or a garage. Do not dismiss concrete so readily; if treated with care and used with imagination, it is a very versatile and strong material equally at home in both modern and traditional gardens.

Concrete is available in almost any colour and even the most stark types quickly weather to give a mellow look, especially when mosses, algae and lichens start covering the surface.

One of the most important qualities of concrete is that its surface finish can be varied to suit your requirements. Have a look at any modern city or shopping centre and you will see that many surface textures are available. By carefully selecting the gravel and sand from which it is made, quite different looks can result. The pebbles in it can be emphasized in the surface, or a smooth, almost polished look can be achieved. The surface can also vary according to the texture of the mould in which the concrete was cast. If wooden planks with a well-marked grain are used, this grain will be transferred to the concrete to give it a wood-like appearance. Even the knot-holes become impressed on the surface.

Concrete can be used either as large cast pieces or as smaller building blocks. Concrete blocks are used in the same way as bricks, being laid in regular courses held together by mortar. They must never be laid dry in the way that some natural stones are, and with any wall over 1.5m (5ft) high some reinforcing is necessary.

As well as simple concrete blocks, generally rectangular in shape, many more interesting shapes and finishes are obtainable. They are not usually much more expensive.

Besides the many solid walling blocks that are available, pierced blocks (often called screen blocks, although they offer little privacy) are another option. These are particularly useful for patio walls or even as dividers between properties where the barrier does not have to be peep-proof.

Pierced blocks are generally light in

colour and, with the strong geometric design formed by the pattern within each block, they make a powerful design element in the garden.

Pierced blocks can be used very effectively in combination with bricks or walling blocks, but as block dimensions vary from one manufacturer to another, check that the units are compatible before you order.

One specialized form of concrete block is a reconstructed stone where the main ingredient is the dust and chippings from natural stone. Such stones are no substitute for the real thing, but are often stronger, much easier to lay, and usually cheaper. It is better to consider them as an alternative material and not a poor imitation. It is best to avoid the type where the surface of a single block has been moulded to look like several different sized stones with mortar between, although even these can be attractive if laid carefully. They are most useful for dwarf walls which will soon be covered with trailing plants.

If concrete is used for large or irregularly shaped structures, it is usually cheaper to buy it already cast. With items such as statues, urns and vases, the concrete is generally cast in one piece. For sheds and coal-stores, each side is cast as a large slab or series of slabs and the whole structure bolted together in your garden. These concrete slabs can be used for fences, for compost bins and for supporting walls on terraces. Larger plant containers are sometimes made from concrete slabs bolted together.

You can easily cast smaller pieces of concrete yourself but larger items need considerable expertise.

Metals, glass and plastics

Iron railings, path-edges, arches, seats and tables as well as steel wire and expanded metal mesh fencing are all well-established in gardens. Unfortunately, metal can be expensive and, unless there is time to look after it properly, it can corrode and rust away quite quickly.

A recent innovation is plastic-covered metal, usually in green, white or black. It can be used for mesh fencing and even for tables and chairs.

Plastics alone are used where their weather resistance or waterproof qualities are required rather than a permanent and heavy-duty structure. Plastics are sometimes used in fences to give a wind-proof viewing panel which is more durable than glass.

Glass, a much older material, is used in most gardens for cloches, garden frames, greenhouses and summerhouses. It is easily broken but is usually longer lasting than most modern plastics.

Above left *Blocks of pierced concrete make an attractive yet sturdy screen for partitioning off different parts of the garden. Sections of the screen are supported by piers (or pilasters) and reinforcing mesh runs through the mortar joints.*

Above *Where a garden overlooks an especially pleasing view, glass or plastic can be inserted into the fence to make an unobtrusive viewing panel.*

CHAPTER 4
MAKING A GARDEN FRAMEWORK

When the contours and layout of your site have been plotted on a flat plan, you can begin to translate the pencilled outlines into proper walls, steps and paved areas which will form the basic skeleton of the garden.

Having planned your garden on paper, the time comes when theory has to be put into practice.

Before you start excavating or ordering materials, transfer the plan from paper to garden, marking out the various beds and features with pegs and string. Proportions, path dimensions and bed sizes can look very different on the ground from on paper. This is your chance to modify the plan if necessary.

Leave the markers in position for several days, looking at the layout from different angles and observing how shadows fall.

This cannot be hurried and whatever you use as markers must be robust enough not to be easily disturbed or blown away. Resist the temptation to further change your plans unless you find it is really necessary to improve the layout.

Where your markers meet an existing feature, a plant or a structure that is to be retained, it is a good idea to mark it specially to prevent accidental removal later. If necessary, protect it with a small fence made of pots or pieces of old wood. Chestnut fencing is very good for this as it is cheap and can be used again elsewhere.

If the plant, particularly a tree or large shrub, requires attention, this is generally a good time to see to it. But do not carry out any pruning at the wrong time otherwise future flowering could be affected, or the tree made vulnerable to certain diseases. If you do decide to prune away dead branches, you can treat the cut surfaces with a wound paint, although there is evidence that this is not always effective.

Remember that really large scale pruning and perhaps bracing of old, large branches requires professional advice from a tree surgeon. However, you should wait until you have noted all trees needing treatment as it will be cheaper to call out the professionals for one big job rather than for several short visits.

Small trees and shrubs that you wish to keep in the garden but not in their present place should be removed, provided it is the right time of year and that you have already prepared a place for them. You should attempt to make ready their final position but if this is not possible because something else is already there, you could try moving them to a temporary position first, although this is best avoided.

Most plants can be moved during the dormant season, from late autumn until spring, unless the ground is frozen. Evergreens are best moved in the separate seasons of autumn or spring.

Plants can be moved at other times, but a general principle is the larger the plant, the less likely it is to survive.

Always move plants in the late afternoon or evening, and always give them plenty of water for several weeks afterwards unless the ground is already very wet.

Do not be tempted at this stage to buy the plants you want. They are much safer in the nursery than on your construction site.

Structures that you wish to keep should be treated just like the plants. They should be protected from subsequent damage, and the opportunity taken to make any repairs that are necessary. It is not wise, however, to apply the final coat of paint at this stage, as it may easily get damaged during construction work, but you should certainly treat all exposed timber and replace any rotten pieces as you come across them.

Structures such as coal stores, dwarf walls or paths that are damaged or well worn should now be re-mortared. Broken bricks, tiles and slabs are best replaced. With badly cracked paving, it is worth considering re-laying all or most of the area. It is much easier to take it up now and start again than to replace individual tiles, setts, cobbles, bricks or blocks.

Any structures that have to be moved or demolished are best taken down. This can be a long and difficult task, as it will be necessary to remove the foundations too.

Opposite *When you are ready to begin preparatory work on your garden site, take care to protect any established areas you do not wish to change. Permanent features will need protecting from the risk of damage, especially if major building tasks are to be undertaken.*

Above *Before its alteration, this town garden was dominated by the curving flower beds and a flight of steps that carried the eye directly towards an unsightly backdrop of neighbouring houses.*

Right *Within five months, the beds had been reshaped into rectangles that reflected the geometric outline of the garden, the lower steps had been widened for greater visual effect and the crazy paving had given way to a covering of washed gravel through which plants could grow. A wooden screen across the back had hidden the view and helped add a sense of privacy.*

However, it is worth remembering that, even if you are not going to re-build elsewhere, the waste materials will almost certainly come in useful later. Small, broken-up pieces of concrete foundation can help to form the foundation for a new path or paved area, and old bricks can be used as curbs or as the base for a barbecue pit, for example. If you intend to re-erect the structure, store the pieces where they are protected from damage. However, it is not usually worth spending a very long time in chipping off every piece of mortar from a brick as new ones are not that expensive.

The stage will be reached when your ideal garden looks like a builder's yard with just a few isolated plants and features standing in their final places. Now is the time to start building the new structures.

Start with the walls, fences, pergolas, arches and other uprights and only then tackle the pavings. If the soil is very muddy or very uneven, it may be useful to lay the path foundations at an early stage to provide easy access to most parts of the garden, but do not lay the final surface until most of the heavy work is finished.

Changing level

The next thing to do is to deal with the inevitable changes of level in your garden. In your original plan you may have decided that the changes could be dealt with by a gentle slope rather than by a series of steps, terraces and retaining walls. Even if your site is perfectly flat, you will probably

For a simple yet dramatic effect, Japanese gardeners have perfected the art of asymmetric deisgns. The raked sand and small mossy mounds above are a feature of the Tofukuji Temple gardens at Kyoto.

their techniques of ground shaping. A low mound in the foreground can obscure an ugly tall building in the distance. Japanese gardeners emphasize the mounds they build by surrounding them with an arrangement of stones or setting them in an evenly raked sand or gravel-scattered surface.

Mounds are also a very useful way of hiding piles of rubbish left by builders or by the demolition of an old wall.

A word of warning – the steeper the mound of soil, the more vulnerable it will be to damage by children, who always seem to be attracted by a slope. To reduce the risk of damage, the slope should be no steeper than 30 degrees. Once the grassed surface is damaged, rain will quickly wash away the soil covering and the carefully shaped mound will become an eyesore. If the mound is steeper than this for any reason, use plants to protect it from wear and tear.

If it is necessary to go up and over a piece of steeply rising and falling ground, a well-built ramp, possibly paved or made of gravel, which can be easily raked back, should be used. When the path is to be used by a pram, wheelchair, tricycle or wheelbarrow, it may be better to re-route it around the base.

If your garden is on a sloping site, such as a hillside, the changes in level may have to be dealt with by terracing. It could even be necessary to have a terrace with its retaining wall right across the plot, but as this is not usually very attractive it may be better to think about a series of overlapping and alternating terraces with steps or ramps in between. By skilful use of winding steps and small walls, quite steep slopes can be concealed and made safer, at the same time providing a range of smaller gardens within the overall design. The side edges of steps can be made less severe if plants can tumble over them, but for safety reasons the front edge should never be hidden.

Terraces with retaining walls and wide flights of steps may be subject to control by your local authority if over 1.2m (4ft) high. If in doubt, it is always sensible to ask your local council or seek professional advice. The council may insist that such structures are built to a statutory specification to prevent accidents. Even lower walls, if their purpose is to retain a considerable weight of soil, especially when it is very heavy because of waterlogging in the winter, should be built with expert advice.

A cheap, easily constructed, long-lasting, readily maintained, very safe and attractive type of retaining wall can be made from old railway sleepers. These can be laid either upright or horizontally and can withstand considerable sideways pressure.

decide that some artificial change of level could add interest and variety to an otherwise monotonous scene.

The eighteenth-century landscape architects reshaped the land into gentle hills and shallow valleys so that it looked like a natural lowland landscape. Often a lake was built, streams diverted and trees planted or re-planted to provide an idealized and romantic pastoral scene from a legendary past. These projects usually involved large scale civil engineering and required many labourers working over a long time. In some cases, whole villages and large farms were re-sited to create a landscape to hide ugly views. In your garden, despite the vast differences in scale, you can achieve similar results by

Sawn-off lengths of telegraph poles sunk into the ground for at least half their length are also very strong and attractive.

Fences

You have probably decided to build a fence around your garden for three good reasons. The most obvious one is that it marks the boundary of your property. Secondly, it serves to keep out unwanted animals such as stray dogs, prevents trespassers entering, and deters 'peeping-toms'. Finally, but most important if you have a young family, it will prevent your children as well as your own pets, from straying on to the road or into your neighbours' gardens. Fences also help to hide ugly views and act as very effective wind-breaks protecting not only delicate plants but making it much more pleasant to sit out in the summer. Even a simple, wide wire mesh fence will reduce wind speeds. If you live in a very windy area, such a fence is less likely to get damaged or blown down than a solid one which must be strong enough to deflect the worst gales.

By shading adjacent parts of the garden from the sun and wind, fences will help to increase the range of microclimates in your garden. In this way you may be able to grow a wider range of plants.

Although a fence may be built of attractive material, such as well-grained timber planks or woven wood strips, and is therefore a decorative feature in its own right, most are generally dull. A long fence may be used to guide your eyes to an attractive feature, such as a tree, at its end but this is not always possible. The only

thing to do with such a fence is to grow plants against it, on it, and over it. Climbing, twining and some rambling plants are suitable but you should not just let them grow all over the fence without some additional support. A mature climber can be heavy enough to topple over an old fence, and a mass of branches and leaves against a fence may retain so much moisture, and attract so many insects and fungi, that it finally rots. By using vine-eyes and galvanized nails with wire stretched between them, or preferably with a light framework just in front of the fence itself, the plants will not rely solely on the fence for their support. However, there is no good excuse for not building a very strong fence in the first place.

Ensure that the uprights, whatever you are going to hang on them, prefabricated panels, planks, or wire-mesh, are firmly and deeply embedded in the ground. As a rule of thumb, all wooden fences over 1m (3ft) high require concrete foundations for the uprights; with a 1.8m (6ft) high fence the foundations should be 75cm (30in) deep at least, and higher ones should be proportionately deeper.

Remember that in most areas any boundary fence over 1.8m (6ft) high may require planning permission if it is likely to obscure the view for drivers. There may also be restrictions to the height of any fencing laid down in covenants in the deeds for the property.

With the post-hole borer, which you can hire from garden centres if you do not own or cannot borrow one, you should first

Below *Horizontal, roughly-hewn boards make up a heavy and strong overlap-type fence.*

Below right *Wide-spaced horizontal timbers make a less weighty looking fence.*

Bottom *An attractive 'triple' combination of low wall, rustic fencing and a hedge.*

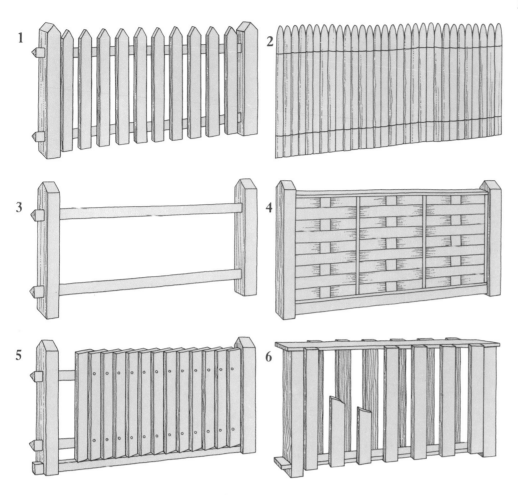

Although the basic design of wooden
fences is the same, the final appearance
can be very different:
1 Picket fence
2 Palisade
3 Post-and-rail
4 Woven panels
5 Feather-boarded
6 Close-boarded

make a hole about 30cm (12in) square, and 10cm (4in) deeper than the foundation depth. In the bottom 10cm (4in) add gravel or small stones to help drainage and then hold the post in place while somebody else pours in the concrete. A suitable mix would be 3 parts coarse aggregate, 2 parts sharp sand and 1 part Portland cement.

Support the post with smaller struts of wood or blocks at its base. Leave them in position for about five days, then remove them and, if it has not been done already, affix the panels, mesh or wire to the posts.

Even if properly treated with preservative, the uprights will probably rot in time and need to be replaced. However, you can avoid this if you use concrete posts into which the panels can be slotted. If the wooden posts are rotten only at the bottom, they can be replaced by short concrete posts, to which the sound wood is bolted. You can also get square-shaped metal supports, into which the uprights are placed and secured.

Walls

Garden walls may serve exactly the same purposes as fences, which are to act as boundaries and screens and to keep people and animals in or out. However, walls are also used much more than fences within gardens to denote changes of use, and to act as visual screens and wind-breaks enclosing sitting-out and play areas.

Walls can be made from natural or reconstructed stone, bricks, or concrete blocks or poured concrete slabs. Usually only one type of material is used for each wall except for the coping on the top and the foundations. All walls over 1.8m (6ft) high are susceptible to damage by gales and, as with fences, may require planning permission from the local council.

One way to reduce costs and still provide

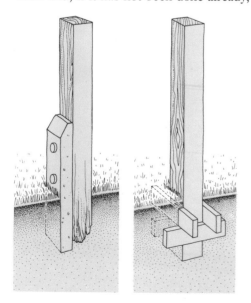

Far left All wooden posts rot in time, but instead of replacing them completely, you can bolt them to short concrete posts.

Left Where damp is not a problem, the posts can be anchored with wooden cleats nailed across the base.

Above *Dry stone retaining walls are often built at quite an angle to the earth behind so that they seem to lean slightly into it rather than act as supports. The angle should be about 50mm in 300mm of height (2in in 1ft), with each stone leaning downwards into the bank of earth to lodge it firmly in place.*

Above right *Large paved areas and patios are generally most successful when only a few different materials are used. Here, soft, brick red and slate grey combine well with the surrounding foliage and simple furniture.*

a strong garden wall is to use an inner core of concrete blocks faced on one or both sides by bricks or natural stones. As already mentioned, decorative concrete blocks can be used by themselves as a substitute for bricks or natural materials.

Although most walls, whatever they are made of, have the spaces between the blocks filled with mortar or cement, it is becoming increasingly popular to build a dry stone wall. Dwarf walls of this kind are very good for growing small rock plants along the top and in the sides. Unfortunately, they often look out of place and require much more skill in building if they are to be stable. To help overcome the stability problem, you could use mortar but wipe the joints out very deeply. The result will closely resemble a dry stone wall.

When laying a rubble wall with the stones laid randomly to give a 'country' look, you must always use plenty of mortar and lay each stone carefully, making sure that all cavities are filled in. The technique is quite different from the almost mechanical and repetitive process of building a brick wall. For the bigger holes you can use smaller stones, such as flints, to help fill the spaces. To improve stability, a pillar of regularly shaped stones or bricks should be built

every 1.8m (6ft). With rubble walls laid in courses rather than randomly, it is necessary to add a short course of even-sized stones every 2-3m (6-10ft).

Brick walls and those made from smoothly finished and regularly shaped ashlar must always be mortared, and great care always taken to ensure that they are upright (retaining walls may need a slight backwards slope). A bricklayer's spirit-level or plumb-bob is a must for this. If you intend to make a really strong and long-lasting wall you must also be sure to use the appropriate mortar.

You can make mortar from ordinary cement, soft sand and lime, but it is much more convenient to buy masonry cement (which already contains a plasticizer to keep the mortar workable for longer) and soft sand. For laying blocks or bricks use 1 part masonry cement to 4 parts sand (3 parts sand for dense masonry blocks or more substantial retaining walls).

The colour of the mortar depends largely on the colour of the sand but you can buy dyes to add to the cement. You must be very consistent with quantities and mixing to avoid varying shades. Try a small area first, and wait until the mortar is completely dry before assessing the colour. Always mix any

dye with completely clean water.

Until you really feel competent at building walls, you should only make a small amount of mortar at a time as it becomes too stiff to use after about an hour. Remember, however, that even if you are very careful, some mortar will be wasted by dropping it on to the ground. Never be tempted to pick it up and use it again as it will be contaminated with soil or dust.

Paths and patios

After building the walls and erecting the fences, tackle the large areas of paving, followed by the paths. The large areas will probably be adjoining the house, where they will be used for sitting out, or at the back or side for play areas, say, and at the front, for a car, caravan or boat. You may also need another fairly large area for standing dustbins and other storage space. If it is a really small garden surrounded by tall trees and buildings, it could be necessary to have more than one paved area so that you can use different ones for shelter or sun depending on the time of day and season of the year.

Large paved areas, commonly called patios, should generally be linked by the path network, but whether they should both be made of the same materials, is a matter of personal preference. Patios can be made from many materials, each having its own features of resistance to wear and tear, ease or difficulty of laying, initial costs, routine maintenance cost, and colours or textures.

Unless you are skilled in garden design and construction, it is usually safer to use as few materials as possible. Combinations of wood and brick, or paving slabs and granite setts, or concrete blocks and cobbles can be very effective if chosen with care and laid well. If poorly chosen and inadequately laid, they can very quickly look incongruous as well as being unsafe.

Whatever the type of paving or path, you must always pay attention to drainage. There is nothing more annoying or unsightly than a large pool of water in the middle of the area. Puddles can also be dangerous, particularly when they turn to ice in winter or get full of slippery, half-rotten leaves in autumn. Paving should always be laid so that it slopes very gently away from the house. If it is a small patio of about 10sq m (12sq yd) there is no need to provide any special drainage channel at the garden edge. Areas larger than this should have a gully leading the water away to the main surface drainage system or into a soakaway. If this is not done, the soil of the surrounding grass or flower beds can easily become waterlogged and the plants will either die or grow very rank and coarse.

Above *Echoing the natural contours of the ground, this curved brick retaining wall is surprisingly graceful.*

Below left *The choice of brick for this patio complements the shape and edging of the pool beyond and makes a formal but stylish sitting out area.*

If the patio adjoins your house, make sure the surface of the paving is at least 15cm (6in) below the level of the house damp-proof course. When the patio is immediately outside a door or a sliding window, you may need to provide a step or even a steep ramp.

All paths and patios must be laid on firm and even foundations. The more wear and tear they are likely to receive and the heavier the loads, the greater the need for firm foundations.

Paving slabs, whether of concrete or natural stone, should be bedded in mortar although, if they are only going to be used lightly, they could be laid on sand. If this is the case, it is essential that the underlying earth is consolidated with a garden roller or by tamping.

If bedding on mortar, prepare a base of hardcore at least 7.5cm (3in) deep, well tamped down until it is quite firm and does not 'give' when you walk on it. You can use broken pieces of brick, concrete and stones, provided they are small enough, bond with ashes, gravel, or small pebbles.

Over the hardcore base spread a 'lean' concrete mix (1 part cement, 3 parts sand) or other fine material such as ash if this is available. Roll or tamp it to bind the materials together.

Trowel the bedding mortar on to the base and carefully lay the paving slabs. You can put mortar between adjacent slabs but a more pleasing result can be had by filling the gaps with sand. To make sure even gaps are left, whether filling with mortar or sand, insert small wooden wedges between each slab, removing them once the underlying mortar has set. Dry sand can then be brushed into the gaps and will serve to drain away surface water. If the path is not going to receive heavy use, you could brush fine soil between the slabs so that small plants can be grown among the paving – but remember that this is also an open invitation to weeds to join them!

Crazy-paving is quite popular, but it is usually uneven. This makes it difficult to keep clean and can spoil the visual effect; most important of all, it can be quite dangerous to walk on. If properly laid, however, crazy-paving can be a satisfactory as well as inexpensive surface. Broken slabs or stones of uneven size are usually much less expensive than whole pieces.

Try to arrange the stones in a random fashion with no continuous joint lines. As edge stones are the most liable to damage, make sure that you use the largest pieces for this; it will also help to keep the outside edges fairly even.

Ordinary red, yellow, or grey wall bricks are traditional materials for paths but in damp areas they quickly become covered with slippery mosses and slimy algae. Unsuitable bricks can also suffer from the effects of frosts, which cause them to flake or crumble. Heavy engineering bricks could be used in their place but they are much too expensive for all but the hardest wear areas, and are not necessary as 'special

Though more time-consuming to lay, paths made of different materials can add a powerful design element to a garden:
1 Stone slabs and bricks of a similar colour have weathered to give a path of attractive yet uniform tones.
2 A brick area has been broken up by strong, straight lines of wood and slate laid on edge.
3 For a wider setting, stone-faced concrete slabs have been both softened and framed by rows of bricks.
4 Granite setts and concrete slabs have produced a simple pattern of contrasting scale and texture.

'quality' bricks will be perfectly satisfactory.

Even better than bricks for paving are brick pavers (sometimes called flexible pavers because of the method of laying). These are thinner than ordinary bricks and have a slightly different surface area which means they can be laid without the gaps that occur with bricks (because of the space left for mortar joints).

Finishing touches

With the backbone of the garden complete, the remaining structural work can be tackled. Garden buildings (a shed or summerhouse, for example) a pergola, or perhaps a pond and garden lighting, can be erected or installed (if you plan carefully, cables can be laid before the paving).

Ideally you should complete all of these fixtures before you start planting, but as plants take some time to become established, once most of the essential and extensive building work is over, do not hesitate to start planting.

Above *The corner of this garden has been converted into a purpose-built dining area with benches, barbecue pit and storage unit. The basic use of only one type of brick reinforces the clean, simple lines of the design and the white, wooden framework of the pergola matches the wooden bench tops and cupboard doors for a functional yet attractive finish.*

Left *The choice of crazy paving for this winding, and informal 'wooded' path matches the mood of the garden perfectly. Laying crazy paving requires much more precision than the name implies: the large, irregular pieces should fit together snugly with as few continuous joint lines as possible.*

CHAPTER 5
DESIGNING WITH PLANTS

Though selecting plants is one of the final stages in planning a garden it is, in many ways, the most important. The right choice will complement the layout, soften the hard lines of the framework and add that vital, personal touch.

Although you will probably have included the names of the plants when you drew up your plan, it is not too late to reconsider your choices. Often the planting list consists of many individual plants included for a variety of reasons, and they may not necessarily provide a good balance. Plants may have been included because you like the fragrance of the flowers, the colour of the fruits, or, perhaps, the autumn leaf colour. Maybe the plant was seen in a garden or at a flower show, and it appealed. Pictures in seed or plant catalogues, or their glowing descriptions, are also a strong temptation.

For impact, however, the borders should be more than a collection of individually desirable plants. It is important to consider how they look together, and to take into account habit, leaf form, and overall impact, as well as the more specific qualities that appeal to you.

More than anything else it will be the plants that give the garden its three-dimensional look, enabling your flat, two-dimensional plan to become a reality. Treat your garden as a block of space with the walls of buildings and fences as its edges, and its lower surface made from the paths, soil and other permanent features. It is the plants that mould this space into attractive shapes, creating special places which you will feel compelled to enter.

The plants that you choose must be those that appeal to you, but they should also be able to reinforce your garden plan. Consider each plant in relation to its neighbours in terms of shapes, sizes, colours, textures and patterns of seasonal growth, so that it becomes integrated into the overall design. This is how a garden can become more of an art form, and can also to some such extent reflect your own particular personality.

There are obviously many approaches to planting design, but generally a planting scheme either tries to control nature by confining bulk planting to beds and borders which have a definite shape, size and position, or it attempts to reflect nature. To achieve a more natural appearance you could even use native plants to try to re-create a woodland, meadow, or heathland scene. Neither approach is wrong and both have many good and bad points. There are good and bad examples of both!

There is another approach, one that allows you to plant a selection of plants which you then view at different seasons to decide whether or not they are suited to a particular position. If they are suitable you keep them, if they are not you can either get rid of them altogether or move them to a better position, replacing them with more suitable plants. This trial and error method can be expensive and takes a long time, but the final result will be plants that really are required both in their own right and as part of the overall scene – as long as you have the resolution to discard failures.

In the confined space of a small garden the 'natural' and the 'controlled' design approaches are not really that different. Even the most formal and precise designs must still succeed naturally and in a re-creation of nature you still have to control the tendency of certain plants to take over and smother the less vigorous species. Self-seeding happens with all sorts of plants and you must try to balance the conflict between removing all the seedlings on one hand, because they upset your plan and, on the other hand, keeping them all because they give a well-established mellow look.

Your design may be fairly formal if the space available will not allow anything else, but there should always be room for one wild patch. This will soon become a focal point in its own right as seasonal changes take place as well as a slow development over the years. Almost certainly the wild patch will attract a selection of insects such as butterflies and moths and also, as would be expected, birds of many kinds. However, if you wish to make a realistic wild garden you must visit a piece of truly wild countryside to see which plants grow in different places and which grow with each other most successfully.

Wild plants grow in natural groupings depending on the climate, soil and history of the area. Over the years, in a wild

Opposite *With the basic framework of your garden established, you can move on to the challenge of choosing plants that will harmonize perfectly with the design and bring your two-dimensional flat plan to life.*

The two plans illustrated here show how to build up a planting design in careful stages. The owners of this small, enclosed garden wanted a 'jungle' effect that could be achieved as quickly as possible. The first plan gives details of the plants they chose for the basic framework, while the second shows the decorative elements they then added.

Framework planting (right)
1 *Hebe anomala*
2 *Pyracantha rogersiana* 'Flava'
3 *Romneya coulteri* (Californian tree poppy)
4 *Hedera helix* 'Goldheart'
5 *Yucca flaccida*
6 *Euphorbia wulfenii*
7 *Choisya ternata* (Mexican orange blossom)
8 *Lonicera japonica* 'Halliana'
9 *Daphne odora* 'Aureomarginata'
10 *Fatsia japonica*
11 *Catalpa bignonioides* 'Aurea' (golden Indian bean tree)
12 *Pittosporum tenuifolium* 'Silver Queen'
13 *Hedera canariensis* 'Varegata'
14 *Taxus baccata* 'Fastigiata' (Irish yew)
15 *Camellia japonica* 'White Swan'
16 *Rhus typhina* (stag's horn sumach)
17 *Viburnum davidii*
18 *Betula papyrifera* (paper birch)

Decorative planting (far right)
19 *Alchemilla mollis* (lady's mantle)
20 *Hydrangea macrophylla*
21 *Caryopteris × clandonensis*
22 *Potentilla fruticosa*
23 *Acanthus mollis*
24 *Rosa* 'Mermaid' (climber)
25 *Nicotiana* (tobacco plant) in summer; tulips in winter
26 *Jasminum nudiflorum* (winter jasmine)
27 *Salvia officinalis* 'Purpurascens' (purple sage)
28 *Rosa* 'Iceberg' (floribunda)
30 *Cortaderia selloana* (pampas grass)
31 *Clematis* 'Madame le Coultre'
32 Herbs

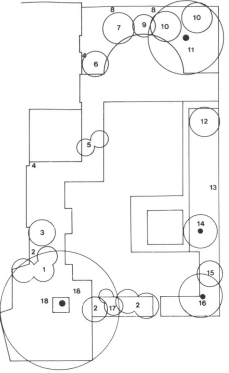
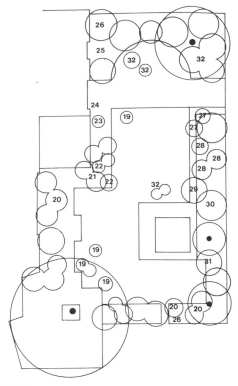

situation, the first colonizing plants eventually become overtaken by later introductions so that, eventually, the most complex vegetation that can be supported remains. In this so-called 'climax' vegetation, there are usually one or two species that dominate the rest of the plants (thus we have oak wood, or heath moor for example), and some of the wild plants appear in large numbers, whereas others are only found as scattered individuals. Bluebells usually cover the ground but only for about three months before the leaves dry up and disappear. As a contrast the gorse bushes scattered on a heathland nearly always have some of their bright yellow flowers on show.

If you intend to make a wild garden always plant the larger plants first. For a woodland effect, plant the dominant trees, then the underlying shrubs and finally the plants of the woodland floor. The lowest layer, the mosses, will follow naturally.

There are three stages or elements of planting in the implementation of all garden designs. The first stage is to establish the garden's basic plant framework of trees and larger shrubs. Next you should provide the bulk of the garden planting against which the third element, the decorative plants, are set. Do not give priority to the decorative plants and then add just a few 'sculptural' larger specimens. Always start with the largest plants to give the general setting for the rest of the garden. Remember, too, that a clump of medium-sized plants grouped together can achieve the same effect as a single large one.

Using trees

Trees always dominate the areas in which they grow, particularly if they have large or unusual leaves or especially bright and abundant flowers and fruits. Weeping willows, ornamental cherries, cedars or perhaps the handkerchief tree *(Davidia involucrata)* all have a very distinctive appearance but can be overpowering when used in a very small garden.

Tree shapes and their leaf textures can create quite distinctive moods. A group of upright trees like Lombardy poplars *(Populus nigra* 'Italica') and the fastigiate beech *(Fagus sylvatica* 'Fastigiata) give a feeling of vigour whereas a weeping willow such as *Salix × chrysocoma* or a birch such as *Betula pendula* 'Youngii' produce a calmer, almost sad, atmosphere. Many trees have associations that reinforce these moods, such as the familiar yew *(Taxus baccata)* which is commonly found in graveyards.

When choosing trees, you must consider their rates of growth and the size they will reach after, say, 30 years. Do not be tempted to choose a vigorous grower that will have to be unnaturally restrained by the continual pruning needed to stop it over-shadowing everything else. Some of the so-called 'dwarf' conifers can be useful plants because they are not really miniature forms but very slow growing, although there are some real pygmies!

The rate of growth of all plants depends partly on their nature and partly on the soil and climate in which they are growing. As a general rule, plants grow more quickly in

damp areas than in dry ones.

Another decision to make with trees is whether to grow deciduous ones (these lose their leaves in autumn), or to concentrate on evergreens. Both have their good points as well as their disadvantages. The best policy is to grow some of each, preferably intermingled. Evergreens tend to be monotonous as they change little from season to season, apart from their flowers and fruits, but they do provide a year-round visual screen as well as an effective windbreak. Deciduous trees are generally more attractive during the warmer months, but are not so good for a shelter or a screen.

Leaf size and shape is important too. Large-leaved trees such as the Indian bean tree (*Catalpa bignonioides*) can be used to reduce the scale of adjoining properties and high walls, whereas plants with relatively small leaves like birches and willows can sometimes give the illusion of making a garden bigger. Round-leaved trees like

limes (*Tilia × europaea* for example) give quite a different effect from those with long narrow leaves like many of the willows.

The feathery leaves of the false acacia (*Robinia pseudoacacia*) and the tropical appearance of fairly hardy palms such as *Trachycarpus fortunei* create their own special atmospheres.

Downy-leaved trees such as the whitebeam (*Sorbus aria*) and those with shiny red leaves like the scarlet oak *(Quercus coccinea)* have their uses.

In the autumn, even the dullest green-leaved trees can turn into torches of red, yellow and orange before their leaves finally fall.

In winter, deciduous trees can be fairly monotonous but there are several varieties that have very attractive barks on trunks and larger branches. Nearly all of the birches have thin, peeling, light-coloured barks, the best being the paper birch (*Betula papyrifera*), but the red-barked ornamental

In this low-maintenance garden, islands of lush foliage are scattered across the basic rectangle of quarry tiles and stone paving. Wild flowers and weeds have been allowed to grow unchecked and the various groups of plants spill haphazardly across the courtyard. In the foreground, a Japanese pagoda tree (Sophora japonica) *is underplanted with thyme, lavender and* Gypsophila repens *while a tamarix dominates the section beyond.*

Above *One of the best-known and most popular of the barberries is the South American* Berberis darwinii. *The holly-like leaves and rich orange-yellow flowers make a superb spring-time display.*

Right *Hornbeam (*Carpinus betulus) *can grow into a sizeable tree but also responds well to clipping into a dense hedge. Although deciduous, its dead leaves remain through the winter while decorative, yellow catkins appear in the spring.*

cherry (*Prunus serrula*) is also very attractive. However, if you really wish to brighten up your garden in winter try the autumn cherry (*Prunus subhirtella* 'Autumnalis Rosea'), which flowers on the bare branches from mid-autumn to mid-spring on all but the coldest days.

Other aspects of trees include the movements they make in the wind. Whole branches of beeches sway like waves in the sea, and the leaves of the aspen (*Populus tremula*) are never still. These movements are often accompanied by gentle, rustling sounds that make these trees even more delightful.

Using shrubs

There may only be room for two or three trees in your garden but no garden is too small for shrubs. These are many-stemmed woody plants that can be deciduous or evergreen, and slow or fast growing.

Many have the virtue of tolerance to pruning to achieve a desired shape. In most cases pruning increases their vigour, though you should take professional advice if you are in any doubt as to where, when and how often to prune. They may not need annual pruning.

Shrubs have as great a range of flower, fruit and leaf colours as do the trees. Their barks include almost the whole range of colours and textures. The red-barked dogwood (*Cornus alba*) has several varieties of garden merit, particularly the brilliant, red-stemmed 'Sibirica' and the shiny, black-purple barked 'Kesselringii'. Several of the willows that can grow equally well as trees or shrubs have brilliant orange, green,

and rubble. Flower colours include purest whites, deep purple-reds, magentas, blues and pale lilacs. Although deciduous and occasionally cut right down to the ground by heavy frosts, it keeps its leaves throughout the winter in sheltered areas.

Shrubs are frequently grown as hedges, which can be clipped to give a formal and symmetrical shape or pruned only occasionally to give a more natural and informal look. Hedge shrubs can be quick-growing such as the hawthorn (*Crataegus monogyna*) Leyland cypress (× *Cupresso-cyparis leylandii*), both of which soon produce an impenetrable screen. Others are much slower, such as the Box (*Buxus sempervirens*), cotton lavender (*Santolina chamaecyparissus*) and lavender (*Lavandula* spp.).

Hedges can be used instead of walls and fences to mark the outer boundaries of your garden, but they are also used for subdividing the garden itself. As a background to a colourful border, hedges could be used much more within a garden than they are. Although technically trees, both hornbeam (*Carpinus betulus*) and beech (*Fagus sylvatica*) can be trimmed to form hedges and are excellent as a foil to a border because they retain most of their dead brown leaves throughout the autumn into late spring. Even the dull privet (*Ligustrum ovalifolium*) particularly if interspersed with the golden privet (variety 'Aurea') has its uses as it generally keeps its leaves throughout the year and will tolerate poor, dry soils. The golden form is an especially attractive plant.

Using climbers and wall plants

Climbing and scrambling plants have two quite different uses in a garden. You may have the problem of an ugly structure that you want to hide rather than spend a lot of time and money on demolishing – a climber scrambling all over it is the solution. The Russian vine (*Polygonum baldschuanicum*) and the ornamental or edible grapes (*Vitis coignetiae*, *V. Labrusca* and *V. vinifera*) are very useful for this purpose as they are such quick-growers once established. Also very good are the scarlet, autumn-leaved Virginia creepers (*Parthnenocissus quinquefolia* and its relatives) and the hop (*Humulus lupulus*).

The other use of climbers is as decorative plants in their own right. The place in the garden where there is no space for a tree or shrub to grow may be ideal for a climbing plant. A light, wooden trellis or arch can be quickly covered with such well-known climbers as clematis. The first to flower in late spring on walls, over sheds and garages and among the branches of the still bare fruit trees is *Clematis montana*

Left *Clematis is one of the most useful and diverse groups of climbing plants. All of them need support of some kind and are ideal for growing on trellis work, pergolas or other wall shrubs.*

or yellow stems. Generally, these colours develop better on new growth and this should be encouraged by cutting away the older stems.

One of the most useful groups of shrubs are the barberries (*Berberis* spp.). Many are armed with prickles that deter dogs, cats and small children, and most thrive in any soil. They either have attractively coloured leaves such as the purple *Berberis thunbergii* 'Atropurpurea' or brightly-coloured flowers and equally attractive fruits such as the orange-flowered, purple-fruited *Berberis darwinii*.

All gardens should include at least one butterfly bush (*Buddleia davidii*) as it is so attractive to butterflies and other flying insects when it is in flower. All varieties will grow in almost any situation, including very shallow and dry soils or among old stones

Above Clematis × jackmanii *'Superba', with fine purple blooms up to 15cm (6in) across, flowers in midsummer.*

Above right *Most of the honeysuckles (*Lonicera *spp.) are vigorous and sweet-scented climbers that will fill the evening air with their fragrance.*

(particularly attractive in its pink form 'Rubens'). It is soon followed by the larger flowered, deep blue or pink Jackmanii hybrids and the delicate-looking species such as *Clematis viticella* and the yellow asiatic types (*Clematis tangutica* and *C. orientalis*). Even the native old man's beard (*Clematis vitalba*) can be grown because, although its flowers are not very spectacular, the feathery-headed fruits are very attractive in the autumn.

For winter interest you could try growing *Rubus cockburnianus* which has purple stems covered with a white waxy bloom (the overall appearance is of white stems). For winter flowers, the winter jasmine (*Jasminum nudiflorum*) is very useful and, in the summer, its close relative *J. officinale* is a must because it is so sweetly scented.

Many gardeners do not approve of variegated or non-green plants as they consider them to be unnatural, but they have many merits. For brightening up a dark corner one of the variegated ivies (*Hedera helix*) such as 'Goldheart', 'Discolor', 'Glacier' and 'Tricolor', or the less hardy but more vigorous and larger-leaved *Hedera canariensis* 'Variegata' (also known as 'Gloire de Marengo') can look particularly good. Golden-leaved forms like *H. Helix* 'Buttercup', and the Japanese honeysuckle (*Lonicera japonica* 'Aure-oreticulata') with its delicate yellow-veined leaves and long-lasting fragrant flowers, are also very useful plants.

Pride of place among garden climbers must be given to the roses. There are hundreds of varieties available today and many more are being introduced into cultivation each year (it is always worth consulting a specialist rose nursery if you can). Most of them produce illustrated catalogues and with roses the camera does not lie – the flowers are usually just as bright and colourful as in their photographs.

Although roses are generally grown only for their flowers, some of them also produce large, bright vermillion hips in the autumn. Roses are deciduous but the extremely vigorous and large flowered 'Mermaid' keeps its shiny green leaves throughout most of the winter. Perhaps the most beautiful of all climbing roses is 'Mme Grégoire Staechelin', which thrives on a north-facing wall and bears heavily-scented, coral-pink flowers shaded with crimson.

An old-established rose of particular use for arches and pergolas is 'Albertine', with its coppery-pink flowers turning brown on the stem quite a time before being shed. Although it requires more support than most climbers, 'Zéphirine Drouhin' is very useful, flowering over a very long period.

You will see from rose growers' catalogues that many favourite hybrid tea roses are also available as climbers. Examples include 'Crimson Glory', 'Gloire de Dijon', 'Mme Butterfly' and 'Shot Silk'.

filipes 'Kiftsgate' is similar and, in some gardens, even more vigorous.

Using herbaceous plants and bulbs

Non-woody herbaceous plants that usually die down in winter after flowering, form the bulk of the planting in most gardens. They can be perennials which means they will grow again next spring, biennials which need two years to complete their life cycle, or annuals that carry out all their functions from seed through germination, growth and flowering, to ripening and shedding their seeds in about nine months.

Bulbs, corms, and tubers are a special type of perennial. Many vegetables are biennials and are harvested in their first year, before they flower. Decorative biennials such as wallflowers (*Cheiranthus cheiri*) and sweet williams (*Dianthus barbatus*) are usually kept in the nursery border and planted out late in their first season to a position where they will flower the following year.

In different climates these differences between annuals, biennials, and perennials may not be so clear-cut. But for garden purposes they should be grown as listed in most books and catalogues.

It is very difficult to give an account of herbaceous plants and their specific uses without producing long lists, but it is reassuring to know that there is always one or more available for any specific purpose in any soil type or microclimate.

Above *'Goldheart' is a distinctive, variegated ivy* (Hedera helix) *with elegantly pointed leaves and attractive colouring.*

Left *Two richly-scented roses, 'Albertine' (a rambler) and 'Zéphirine Drouhin' (a climber) enhance the old-world atmosphere of this cottage garden.*

Rambling roses are better grown over arches and other frameworks as they are liable to become mildewed if there is not much air circulating around them. Their flowers are usually smaller than those of climbers, but there are generally many more of them. Probably the best known is the blush pink 'Dorothy Perkins', which is also available with a deep crimson flower (variety 'Excelsa'). The most vigorous rose of all is the rambling 'Wedding Day' with very fragrant, creamy-yellow flowers soon becoming white as they open. It will grow up to 5m (16ft) in a single season. *Rosa*

Even in one group of herbaceous plants, for example the chrysanthemums, daffodils, or dianthus, there are many separate species each with its own preferences and garden uses. As well as increasing the range of flower colours, plant breeders also aim to change the behaviour of herbaceous plants. You can now buy chrysanthemums that can be grown as house plants, as greenhouse specimens for the cut flower market, and as outdoor border plants. Chrysanthemums of one type or another are now available to produce flowers throughout the year.

Early-flowering daffodils such as 'February Gold' and 'Peeping Tom' extend the daffodil season from late winter to late spring.

Another example of the plant breeders' work is the sweet pea (*Lathyrus odoratus*) which is now available in any flower colour other than true yellow, either as a tall, vigorous, herbaceous climber or as a dwarf border plant.

It is a good idea to write down the names and features of plants you see in a garden or read about in a catalogue but, before you finally decide to buy any, check again in a reference book to make sure they are suitable for your soil and site. This checking is important because if one plant was, say, a half hardy annual, it would not be suitable for planting out until all danger of frost was over.

Your list of plants should be divided into groups based on their features. You could list them according to flower colour, scent, height, or cost. But it is probably better to list them under their possible garden uses.

Make a special note of plants that have a well-defined shape such as the giant rhubarb (*Gunnera manicata*) and some of the spurges (for example *Euphorbia wulfenii*). Plants of this type are called 'architectural' or 'sculptural' plants.

A very useful list can be made of plants that can be depended on to succeed in almost any garden. They may be common plants or much rarer ones, but the quality they have in common is that they are guaranteed to flower each year whatever the weather. The garden cranesbills (*Geranium* spp. – not to be confused with the indoor, scarlet geraniums, correctly called pelargoniums) are very dependable and available in a range of colours. Russell lupins (*Lupinus polyphyllus*), day lilies (*Hemerocallis*), Japanese anemones, plantain lilies (*Hosta* spp.), and red hot pokers (*Kniphofia* spp.) are also reliable.

Decorative vegetables can form an unusual group. Asparagus, ornamental beetroot, globe artichoke, maize and red and variegated cabbages, are all distinctive.

All of these can be eaten as vegetables but are equally at home in the flower border. Culinary herbs form another group of plants equally at home in the flower garden or vegetable patch. Marjoram (*Origanum vulgare*), sage (*Salvia officinalis*), tarragon (*Artemisia dracunculus*), and any of the mints could be put into the list.

Another useful category is plants for special conditions, such as damp sites. This list should include the double buttercup (*Ranunculus acris* 'Flore Pleno'), globe flower (*Trollius* spp.) and monkey flower (*Mimulus luteus*). Other lists could be for pollution-resistant plants or those suitable for cold and exposed sites or the salt-laden air of the seaside.

Ground cover plants

A trend in gardens today is not to have patches of bare earth between plants but to use low-growing scramblers or mat-forming plants as a ground cover. The advantages of these are that weeds are suppressed once the ground cover is established, therefore reducing the tiring tasks of hoeing and hand weeding. The taller plants may benefit from a permanent, moisture-retaining 'mulch' around their roots. Ground cover plants are also attractive in their own right, often bearing colourful flowers or decorative leaves.

Lawns are a form of ground cover using a wide variety of grasses, many of them especially bred for this purpose. However, in the Middle Ages lawns were often made with other plants such as thyme (*Thymus serpyllum*) and chamomile (*Chamaemelum nobile*, syn. *Anthemis nobile*). These are not as hard-wearing as grass, and are difficult to weed and maintain but, when they are walked on, the crushed leaves release a very pleasant perfume.

In rose borders and between small shrubs, the Russian comfrey (*Symphytum grandiflorum*), St John's wort (*Hypericum*), epimediums, and periwinkles (*Vinca major* and *V. minor*) establish themselves very well. If the taller plants are close together and cast deep shade, you should consider a ground cover plant that naturally grows on the floor of woodlands. *Pachysandra terminalis* and the yellow deadnettle (*Galeobdolon luteum*) can be used. Damp soils can be covered well with creeping jenny (*Lysimachia nummularia*), or with any of the many forms of bugle (*Ajuga* spp.) that are available.

You should experiment to see what will grow as ground cover in your garden. Even those plants that you normally consider to be weeds may become acceptable if they are not too vigorous or do not spread to other parts of your plot.

By choosing plants that fit together in a unified colour scheme – blue with white and pink with grey for example – or those that have strong leaf shapes and textures, a herbaceous border can be turned into a striking design feature.

CHAPTER 6

GARDEN FEATURES

Your choice of furniture and decoration will create a very individual atmosphere in your garden and, according to your lifestyle, you can turn it into a calm retreat, an outdoor dining room or a children's play area.

Walls, fences, plants, and paving will give a garden its basic shape and character, but the finishing touches like garden furniture, lighting, or perhaps a fountain or a pergola will make it look complete.

Tables and chairs for sitting out, a pool where you can enjoy the pleasures that water brings, a greenhouse, a garden-shed, interesting plant containers, and garden lights are all possibilities. Obviously any project that involves mains electricity in the garden calls for professional help but you can install low-voltage lights and pumps yourself (the transformer is kept indoors and only a low-voltage cable is used outside). All the other projects should be within the scope of a keen do-it-yourselfer.

Whatever the garden feature you tackle, there are two important principles: plan exactly what you require before you start, and try not to compromise on the quality of materials you use. Buy the best materials within your budget. This does not necessarily mean that you have to buy new materials, as old ones may often be as good. However, you must always be wary of 'special offers' at ridiculously low prices. The initial result may appear satisfactory but the feature may only have a short life. A good example would be a very cheap greenhouse which might last only a few years. Also remember that, if you do not have the money now, many of the garden features can be added from one year to the next over quite a period of time.

Pergolas

A pergola is essentially a series of arches linked together, generally over a paved area but frequently along a walkway of any type. The upright supports and the overhead beams can be all of the same size and material, but usually it is the 'roof' which is emphasized. An overhead framework gives the illusion of more floor space than there really is and, therefore, a pergola is a very useful feature for a small garden.

A pergola can be free-standing within the garden, or it can adjoin the home like a patio-overhead, to form a half-way point between an indoor sun-lounge and the outdoor garden itself. It will provide some shelter and shade as well as being a place on which plants may grow. A pergola could also be considered as a very cheap type of house extension.

Of course, a pergola is not much help in really bad weather, but a well-made one with a good covering of plants will let you sit and even eat out-of-doors from mid-spring to mid-autumn. If the pergola is south facing and enclosed on two or three sides by the house walls or boundary fences, it could even be quite pleasant to sit there on bright winter day.

Pergolas are very useful design features to include if a house has a monotonous outside wall or has a very irregular outline. Built along a straight wall, the inclusion of a pergola makes an easy way to disguise the dullness, particularly once it is covered with climbing plants. In the same way, odd spaces between walls and a shed or garage can be brought into use.

Where a pergola is built alongside the house, the adjoining indoor room can be floored with a material similar in colour and texture to that used under the pergola itself, so that a sense of 'unified space' is achieved. In the summer, the difference in being 'indoors' or 'outdoors' would seem to disappear, again giving the illusion of more space. However, you should remember that the outdoor paved area will be subject to very bad conditions in the depths of the coldest and wettest winters: it should be frost resistant, non-slippery, and laid with a slight fall to shed water so that a pool does not form on it.

If the pergola is to be built next to your house, it will look better if it is designed to reflect the materials of the building. If the house is made of brick, for example, the pergola supports should be brick also, though metal is quite acceptable with many materials. You should also make sure that the pergola bears some relationship to the lines of the adjoining window and doors. As a general rule, the top of the pergola should be just above the lintel of the ground-floor window or door frame.

If you are having a new house built, it

Opposite *A delightful corner has been created in this garden by using two simple features: an arbour of roses and a decorative stone vase.*

Above *A pergola can be built as an extension to the house or to make a shady retreat in the larger garden.*

Above right *A paved yard can be brightened up by a display of shrubs and summer bedding annuals planted in suitable containers.*

might be worth trying to persuade the builder to extend outside the upstairs floor beams to form the overhead timbers of the pergola.

If you have small children make sure that the pergola does not become an easy route from an upstairs bedroom! Nevertheless, it should always be a strong structure and not just a set of poles or planks loosely nailed together. Ideally, it should be able to support a child's swing or an adult hammock.

The pergola itself generally looks better when it is a fairly plain structure without too much ornamental brickwork; it is the plants that grow on it that give its particular qualities. Occasionally, it may be difficult to design a plain pergola to look right – say, alongside a house which is old and highly ornate. In this case a trellis can be used to considerable effect.

Using containers and ornaments
Although most of your plants will be in the garden itself and planted in the soil, there is always room for plants in containers. Most greenhouse plants and indoor pot-plants will benefit from some time out-of-doors in a sheltered space during the summer. These can be arranged and re-arranged at will to suit the mood of the garden and to make the most of what is available.

There are also plants that grow better outdoors, if kept in pots or larger containers (sometimes referred to as 'planters'). Some plants only flower and fruit well when their roots are restricted. The best known example of this is the edible fig (*Ficus carica*) which fruits very well when grown in a sawn-off wooden barrel or large urn.

When grown in the garden, the position of a plant is fixed but displays in a planter can be moved to the most appropriate spot for each season. Planters are also very useful for growing plants in parts of the garden where there is no soil or where it would be difficult to have an open flower bed of any size.

It is possible to buy a wide range of pots and planters, but you can have fun making them yourself. An old coal-scuttle, chimney-pot or wheelbarrow can be used as long as there is some outlet hole for surplus water to drain away. If you are lucky enough to have an old stone sink or even a newer type glazed earthenware one, you could create a miniature landscape by making a sink garden of dwarf plants.

Plant containers need not always have plants in them to be attractive in a garden. They can be treated as 'sculptures' and in many ways are more appropriate than many of the modern glass-fibre or concrete replicas of classical statues. Modern abstract sculpture or carefully placed boulders and unusually shaped driftwood can be used, but brightly-painted garden gnomes or decorative features need more thought before they are introduced.

Water in the garden

Water features have been used in gardens for well over two thousand years. Sometimes you may be lucky enough to have a natural pool or even a small stream running through your plot. If you are particularly fortunate you may even have a river or canal at the bottom of your garden, though this is unlikely.

In such cases however, remember that you must not divert the water flow or enlarge a river bed or bank without permission from the local water authority. It is not only illegal but could have an effect on the river's ability to cope with flood water. Also, you should not pump water out of a river or canal to irrigate your garden or to fill your pond unless you have obtained permission beforehand. In most areas, too, you will require a special licence to use a hose-pipe or garden sprinkler with mains water, even if only a couple of times a year.

As well as being decorative, a garden water feature can serve the useful purpose of lowering the air temperature around it on a hot day. A pool placed in your overall garden design serves not only as a focal point but as a line between other features. Water can create a variety of moods both in your garden and in the users of the garden. An upright, spouting fountain gives a sense of vigour and continuing energy whereas a very still pool, with a glass-like surface reflecting the water-side plants, suggests something very tranquil and contemplative.

A gently bubbling flow, even though powered by an electrical circulating pump, may recall a range of early childhood memories. Today the sound of a gurgling water feature can camouflage the noise of the traffic and industry outside and may even drown the sound of neighbours.

The combination of plants and design features such as containers or figurines can be used to add a decorative touch on the small or grand scale and can be simple or highly ornate.

Elegance is the keynote in this classically designed patio which combines a unified planting scheme with the coolness of a small water garden and white-painted furniture.

There are certain rules to remember when siting a garden pool. Water should always have some direct sunlight on most of its surface for at least an hour each day, preferably for much longer. Water plants require good light to enable them to grow and flower.

Ideally, pools should not be too near trees that drop large numbers of leaves in the autumn. Grass-clippings, dead leaves or any other organic matter must not be allowed to accumulate in a pool because

they quickly foul the water and make it unsuitable for plants and fish. Never use a pool to clean or rinse garden tools and never shake out a fertilizer bag over it in the hope that this will help the plants.

When a pool is first made and stocked, you will find that for some time it will look quite unnatural being either very clear or very cloudy. However, sooner or later it will settle down and the clear water become slightly cloudy or the very cloudy water become clearer. In hot weather it may suddenly become murky almost overnight only to become very much clearer just as suddenly a few days later. This is because minute single-celled plants called algae multiply very rapidly when the conditions are right but die off quickly when they have used up their food supply. However, you need not worry as these natural processes gradually lead to a 'balanced' environment in your pool where the plants, snails and fishes are all living in harmony.

To encourage the natural balancing of a pool you should first of all plant plenty of submerged oxygenating plants, preferably in the plastic mesh baskets sold for this purpose (clay flower pots can be just as good but tend to topple over more easily). Also try to introduce plants with floating leaves, such as water-lilies, as soon as possible, as the reduced light reaching the water below will also help to inhibit the algae that cause green water. At this stage you can add water snails and water insects. But there is no need to go to much trouble; before long various types of water beetle will have found their way into your pool.

It is best to wait for about a month after planting before introducing any fish. Although large specimens of Japanese Koi carp are very expensive, small ones are much cheaper and they grow quickly. Goldfish, too, are bright and interesting even though they lack the spectacular colouring and size of Koi carp, and they are much cheaper.

Do not be tempted to overfeed any type of fish: in a well-balanced pool with adequate and variable planting there will be enough insects and other pool life to make it unnecessary to feed them at all for most of the year (except, perhaps, early autumn).

Try not to overstock the pool. As a rough guide, one medium-sized fish for every square metre of water surface is about right. If there are more than this they will suffer in the summer when high water temperature will reduce the dissolved oxygen content just at the time when the fish are at their most active and, therefore, require most oxygen.

Pools can be formal or natural-looking. A formal pool with a square or rectangular shape, for example, is useful in some gardens as it lends itself to being sited in almost any position, whereas a natural pond is more limited in this respect. A formal pool can be raised above the general garden level and its surrounds can be used as a seat. This is a useful feature as it reduces the chance of small children falling in.

Never leave very young children or very old and infirm grown-ups near any pool unless they are under supervision.

An informal pool is probably the cheaper

to make as you can readily buy pre-formed plastic shapes to place in a pit dug out beforehand and lined with damp sand. Alternatively you can use a flexible pool liner; these easily adapt to the contours of an informal shape, though it is wise to avoid tight or unnecessary curves. To finish it off the top edges are best covered with paving slabs.

Garden buildings

Unless they are very large, permanently fixed to the walls of your house, or that of a neighbour, or sited in the front garden, you do not need planning permission from your local council for any garden building. Nevertheless it is always worth enquiring from the local planning officer to make sure you are not breaking any regulations. Some buildings are covered by building regulations, but those provided by a reputable company should meet the specifications.

Greenhouses, conservatories, summer-houses and garden sheds can all be bought ready-made, generally in kit-form – all you have to do is to bolt them together, although you may have to provide the foundations.

Before deciding which to buy, send for as many different manufacturers' catalogues as possible. List the features you would

A generously sized, but informal, pool fits naturally into its lush surroundings while the small pool-side statue makes a delightful focal point right at the water's edge.

Above *Storage can be a problem in a garden and the addition of a small shed may prove a great asset. There are many different styles to choose from but most will need fitting out with some shelves, hanging racks and a work surface or table.*

like, including size, shape, ease of erection and special facilities as well as cost and the annual maintenance required. Then consult all the catalogues and see as many as possible of the buildings erected at the manufacturer's showground or garden centres. Do not always buy the cheapest model; it may not last long and may be very difficult to adapt to your own special requirements.

The most important building must be the shed in which you store your garden equipment, perhaps your seeds and, if it is frost-proof (very few are!) some of your crops like apples and potatoes. If you have garden tools of reasonable quality, they deserve adequate protection.

Shelves, racks, a work-top and storage bins should be found in all toolsheds, though these are features that you will probably have to add yourself. As some tools like powered mowers will be heavy, you should avoid having steps by the door. Otherwise, it is helpful to keep a wide plank of wood handy so that you can push the mower in easily.

After a shed, the most useful garden building is a greenhouse. It can be used solely to bring-on seedlings for summer bedding, followed by tomatoes and cucumbers until early autumn, However, most greenhouses also attract many other 'occupants' and are used for all sorts of other purposes, not all connected with growing plants! A deck-chair in a heated greenhouse in winter is an ideal retreat

from a busy house! Greenhouses are used as a hospital for sick house-plants, a place to keep a collection of cacti and succulents, to produce extra-early pickings of daffodils and other spring flowers, and to house tender summer crops such as aubergines, peppers, and melons.

Greenhouses can be free-standing or 'lean-to'. A free-standing greenhouse might be easier to fit into the overall garden design. Traditional greenhouse shapes are not particularly attractive, but this will not matter if you can find an inconspicuous position (avoid tucking it away at the end of the garden – providing a power supply and water will be more of a problem).

Some less traditional designs, such as dome-shaped and octagonal greenhouses can be made into a feature, even on a patio.

A lean-to may provide less favourable growing conditions for some plants, but because it is likely to be against the house it is likely to be used more. Some modern lean-to greenhouses are almost like conservatories.

If you can afford one, a conservatory or sunroom is a very valuable addition to any house. Although they are meant mainly for people, conservatories are ideal places to grow plants. You can create a tropical-looking scene in which you are cut off from the outside world. Or you can stock it with palms, ferns, and aspidistras and pretend you are back at the turn of the century!

If space or money are the limiting factors, you can always make a 'picture-

Right *Modern metal-framed greenhouses can be put up quite easily. If possible, the greenhouse should be placed on open ground, away from the main part of the garden but within reach of both power and water.*

Above left *At one time conservatories were the height of fashion and even town houses were graced with the addition of tiny, attractive sun rooms of distinctive style.*

Above *If a conservatory can be built against a brick wall which faces the sun, it will make an ideal place for growing tender plants and exotic trees.*

window' or 'plant-window' in which plants are grown either inside or outside the house window in a miniature greenhouse attached to the frame.

For a sheltered sitting-out space, a summerhouse can be surprisingly cheap and extremely versatile. You can treat a summerhouse as a building half-way between a greenhouse and a shed and, if it is large enough, it can be used for growing a selection of plants as well as storing garden equipment and providing a place to sit almost throughout the year. Do not expect plants to do very well, however. A summerhouse can be very hot or very cold in comparison with the home, and the light cannot compare with that in a greenhouse.

A summerhouse may be placed anywhere in a garden, but ideally it should receive sunlight for most of the day. Some shelter from the hottest mid-day summer sun is useful and it should not be in a very windy space. In order to make the most of the sunlight in smaller gardens, summer-houses can be built on a base which can be rotated to face the sun at different seasons of the year. This, however, is a very complex job and needs professional advice.

Garden lighting

Garden lighting is usually installed for the very practical reason of illuminating a garden path, gate, porch, or patio. It is always useful to have lighting in a garden

shed or greenhouse. However, outdoor lights can be pretty as well as practical. And they can enable you to enjoy your garden when it is dark, and not just during the day.

As well as being very friendly and welcoming, it is helpful to have good lighting for garden paths, particularly where there is little or no street lighting. There is no need to install a full-sized, lamp-post – you can get a range of short-pillared lighting fitments. They usually have a reflecting shade which throws the light on to the ground in a wide circle so that you can see where you are walking without everything else being illuminated. To avoid excessive glare, they can also be fitted with frosted-glass shades.

If the main aim is to light an outside sitting area, there are many waterproof light fittings obtainable from larger garden centres and some electrical goods shops. Individual plants can be illuminated to emphasize their colour, leaf-shapes or textures. A single rotating spot-light is useful for this and its use is not confined to plants – a soft light playing on a frosty winter scene can be very effective.

Do not be tempted to bathe your garden with festoons of multi-coloured lights strung permanently across the trees. They rarely do more than bleach out the natural colours of the plants around them.

The secret of many of the really successful garden lighting schemes is to

Above *The dramatic effects of garden lighting can be used in a variety of ways. Bright colours will make decorative features in their own right, while plain fittings can be concealed among tall shrubs and trees to cast patterns through the foliage or provide stronger illumination below.*

ensure that the light source is hidden. A single beam of light shining on a statue or boulder, or on the surface of a pool can create an impressive as well as mysterious atmosphere.

It cannot be stressed too highly that all electrical light fittings used out of doors must be suitable for the job. Ordinary domestic fittings must not be used. All outdoor fittings must be waterproof and strong enough to withstand many more knocks than indoor types.

All electric wiring should be installed professionally, unless you are using a low-voltage system. Even if you feel sufficiently experienced to wire the lamps yourself, you

should get the whole system approved by a qualified electrician before you use it.

For a temporary effect or occasional use, it is not necessary to use electricity to light your garden. A range of bottled gas light fittings are available and, although they are not so decorative, they are very powerful and friendly for illuminating a barbecue or outside sitting area.

To create a romantic atmosphere, oil-lamps, flares and candles can be used. If you have a pool, try floating lit candles on pieces of wood. Always remember, however, that great care must be exercised if children or pets are around where there are hot surfaces or unguarded flames. Caution is

weather resistance. You can always take the furniture in and out of doors as you require it, but this is not practicable with items that are very heavy or require a lot of storage space.

The folding, traditional, brightly-striped canvas wooden deck-chair is always acceptable and easily stored. An alternative arrangement is to have the basic furniture outdoors all the time and just bring cushions and table coverings indoors when they are not needed.

Before finally deciding on the type of chair you want, you should think about how you will use it. If eating outdoors is likely to be the main use, upright chairs will be best. Deeply reclining loungers are most unsuitable for this, but they are ideal for sunbathing.

If you have robust trees in your garden, the old-fashioned hammock can make a very simple all-purpose seat, although you need to be fairly nimble to get in and out of it!

Most garden centres and departmental stores offer a range of different swinging seats and settees, usually with protective awnings to match.

Wood is a popular material for outside furniture and will last many years provided you remember to treat it with an annual coat of linseed oil, wood-preservative, or paint, depending on what was used on the original surface.

A really big wooden table is useful in any garden. A brightly-coloured tablecloth will quickly turn it into a picnic table, but for the rest of the time it can be used as a work-top or play surface.

The most durable of all garden furniture is that made from stone, brick, or concrete. It is not so comfortable as wood, being hard and cold in cool weather and hard and hot in the summer. However, it has the advantage of needing little or no maintenance and is easy to clean. If you have a barbecue area, brick or stone are the most suitable materials as they are least affected by the oil and fat that accompanies much outside eating.

Finally, do not assume that good garden furniture is only really for sophisticated gardens or wealthy gardeners. Many very serviceable, tough and attractive items can be made by the average do-it-yourself enthusiast. Make sure you use good timber and rust-proof nails, and always treat the wood with an appropriate preservative followed by a coat of linseed oil, (or if painted, a primer plus two undercoats before applying the top gloss). If you are not that good at carpentry, many items of garden furniture can be bought as easy-to-assemble kits at prices lower than ready-made pieces.

Left An informal garden setting is best matched by simple furniture and, if this can be built around existing features, it will make the placing look more natural. Furniture that will be constantly exposed to the elements should be made of sturdy materials (slatted surfaces are also practical as they allow rain water to drain off) while more delicate fittings should be brought indoors during bad weather.

also needed if such lighting is used during the summer months, when hot spells may have left nearby plants tinder-dry or, of course, if it is a windy evening!

Garden furniture

As 'outdoor living' has increased so has the range of outdoor furniture available to enable you to enjoy it. The choice of furniture should be influenced by the style of your garden. Tubular metal or moulded plastic is suitable for the ultra-modern garden but wickerwork is better for the more traditional retreat. Price and availability are important too, of course, but also take into account durability and

CHAPTER 7

SAMPLE PLANS

All gardens are different in the problems they pose and the way they are planned and planted. From rooftops and balconies to a fully productive vegetable plot, the following pages illustrate the scope of design possibilities for almost any site.

Good design ideas often spring more readily to mind if they are developed from existing examples. Someone else's solution to a problem may suggest a modification that would help to solve a similar problem in your own garden.

A plan for someone else's garden can never be taken as a whole for your own; size, aspect, and soil are all likely to be different. But they can serve as a source of inspiration.

This final chapter shows you how other people have created their own successful gardens on a range of sites. Most of these sites presented some difficulties, and most of the owners had their own special requirements. Most of them also had a good idea of the sort of garden they wished to make and the atmosphere they wished to establish.

The sites covered by these plans range from a very steep slope to a flat penthouse roof, while individual requirements range from a herb garden to a jungle-like retreat in the middle of a city.

There is usually one central feature or focal point in each plan. Sometimes it is a plant or group of plants, but it is often a structure such as a pool.

You will get plenty of ideas from looking at these plans, but bear in mind that not only are no two sites identical, and that each individual will have different requirements, but also that no two garden designers, professional or amateur, will have the same solutions to the problems. Each garden shown is unique, in the same way that your garden is unique to you.

Hopefully each garden here has one feature you could adopt, but you must always make sure that your garden is designed as a complete entity and is not just a motley collection of other people's ideas.

Besides these illustrated gardens, it is always worth visiting any site 'in the flesh': it does not matter if it is large or small, private or public, good or bad (you will know what you want to avoid!). Visit places not only in late spring and during the summer months but also in the autumn and winter to see how they rate as all-year-round designs.

Remember that you will have to look out on your garden almost every day of the year and it should have something attractive and interesting in it at all seasons. Whenever possible, speak to the owners of the gardens you see to find out what the plots were like beforehand. Do not be afraid to inquire if their gardens are really what they wanted to achieve when they started out.

Let them tell you of the problems they have faced and how they have tried to solve them. There are booklets published that list all the major gardens of interest but you should not confine yourself to these. If you see an interesting or unusual garden anywhere, the owner may be pleased to show you around and talk about it.

Nowadays many of the big flower shows, such as that held in London, at Chelsea (in May), feature small gardens designed for particular clients or inspired by a particular theme. Some of these gardens are really no more than a good excuse to exhibit a large number of flowering plants often at unusual times, while others are filled with so many features that they could never be lived with. However, most of them are very good samples of the work of current garden designers and show what can be achieved in a short time provided you know clearly beforehand what you want to do. Unfortunately most of them require much more labour than you could provide to give their 'instant' effect, but they could be built by one person over a couple of years.

Old meets new

The great problem the owners, a young couple with a small child, faced with their garden was that it was only part of the original garden. The original eighteenth-century mansion was split up some time ago to form smaller dwellings and, so that each household had a plot of its own, the large garden was subdivided as well. Their piece was partly enclosed by a very high, south-facing wall covered with an old trellis and a well-established ivy. The working parents wanted a garden that required very little routine maintenance but would be suitable for their child to use at all times.

Opposite *Before settling on a design for your garden, it's always worth looking at the way other people have tackled the problem. Many useful ideas can be gleaned this way and, even if you do not want to follow a particular scheme exactly, you can pick out the themes that appeal to you or adjust the various features to suit your needs.*

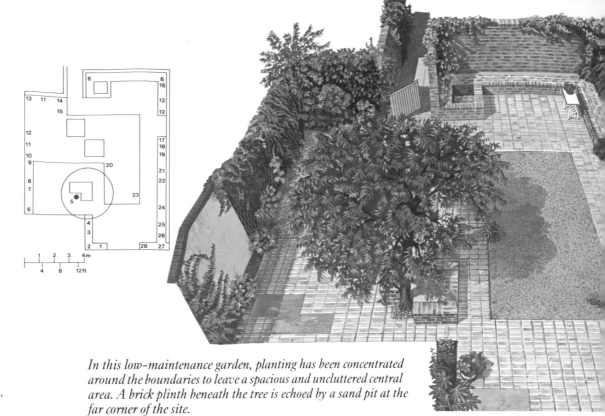

In this low-maintenance garden, planting has been concentrated around the boundaries to leave a spacious and uncluttered central area. A brick plinth beneath the tree is echoed by a sand pit at the far corner of the site.

There was a very small, stone-paved area already and this has been extended by using bricks similar in colour and texture to those making the south-facing wall. The large central area was covered by local gravel. At the edge, against a wall, were added a few plants of bamboo (*Arundinaria murielae*) and self-seeding, single-flowered hollyhocks (*Althaea rosea*) to provide seasonal colour and movement. Across the gravel, 'stepping stones' were made of small brick-paved squares.

The only significant plant in the garden when the owners arrived was a tall box elder (*Acer negundo*). This was retained and became the focal point, enhanced by building a brick plinth around part of the base of the trunk. This plinth is now used for sitting out and as a ledge for potted plants in the summer. The tree had very few low branches as the previous owners had lopped them away in the past. The result is a very useful 'umbrella' which is only penetrated by the heaviest showers in summer.

An unfortunate feature of the garden is that, for most of the year, it is far too shaded for many plants to develop their full potential. The decision was therefore made to concentrate on plants with distinctive forms and evergreen leaves in a variety of shapes and textures. One advantage of this is that the garden has colour and interest around the year and provides an attractive outlook from the house. For the odd splash of spring and summer colour, containers have been arranged around the terrace and these can be planted up with spring bulbs and annuals as required.

Above left *Planted in the gravel bed along a sunless wall is the graceful bamboo,* Arundinaria murielae. *Bright splashes of colour are provided by self-seeded hollyhocks* (Althaea).

Above *Interest is maintained throughout the year because of lush, evergreen planting. Here, the dark green foliage of* Choisya ternata *and* Euonymus radicans *contrast well with the variegated ivy.*

Left *The garden is linked to the path beyond by neat brick stepping stones across an area of gravel broken by the occasional plant.*

Some summer colour was possible at the end of the garden furthest from the house but, because this was the sunniest corner, it was decided to use the area for sitting, outdoor eating and sunbathing. A wide brick-bench seat with a raised sandpit was also built. When the child grows up, the pit can be used for barbecues or, perhaps planted with some summer annuals.

In all parts of the garden different types of climber have been encouraged to scramble over the walls. The result is that, after only three years, vigorous growers like ivy, clematis and jasmine already look as if they had been there for much longer.

Above *The miniature elegance of a window box contrasts with the rampant growth of a Virginia creeper which both covers the dull brick wall and provides a showy autumn display.*

Right and far right *Set against plain, white timber, strong foliage plants dominate this paved garden. Contrasting leaf shapes and colours provide a wealth of interest, especially in the shaded corner leading up to the house.*

A city jungle

There is always noise in the city and it is not possible to block it out completely. However, if all movement can be disguised and a tropical-look achieved it becomes quite easy to forget where you are once you relax in this sort of garden.

Like a true tropical jungle, the emphasis is not on flower colour but on a wide variety of plant and leaf sizes, shapes and textures.

The plants were also chosen for their different shades of green foliage. Access to the garden is from the house through a high level door and down a few steps. White timber steps and rails blend with the house cladding and emphasize the greens of the 'jungle' plants. There is also another entrance from the street along a narrow passage. To add interest to this route an old

cannon has been partly restored and is used as a piece of sculpture. Whichever way you enter the garden, you find yourself in a tropical, green room.

The garden is furnished very simply with white painted chairs, which again echo the house cladding and the steps.

The centre of the garden is paved with concrete slabs of several, very pale colours. The planting around it is not really as unplanned as the word 'jungle' would suggest. The position of each plant was drawn on the plan beforehand. A focal point is the bamboo (*Arundinaria japonica*) and the small pond next to it.

Cordyline australis, a spiky plant, and the palm *Trachycarpus fortunei* add to the jungle look. The raised bed in the centre has a very vigorous juniper and a couple of the

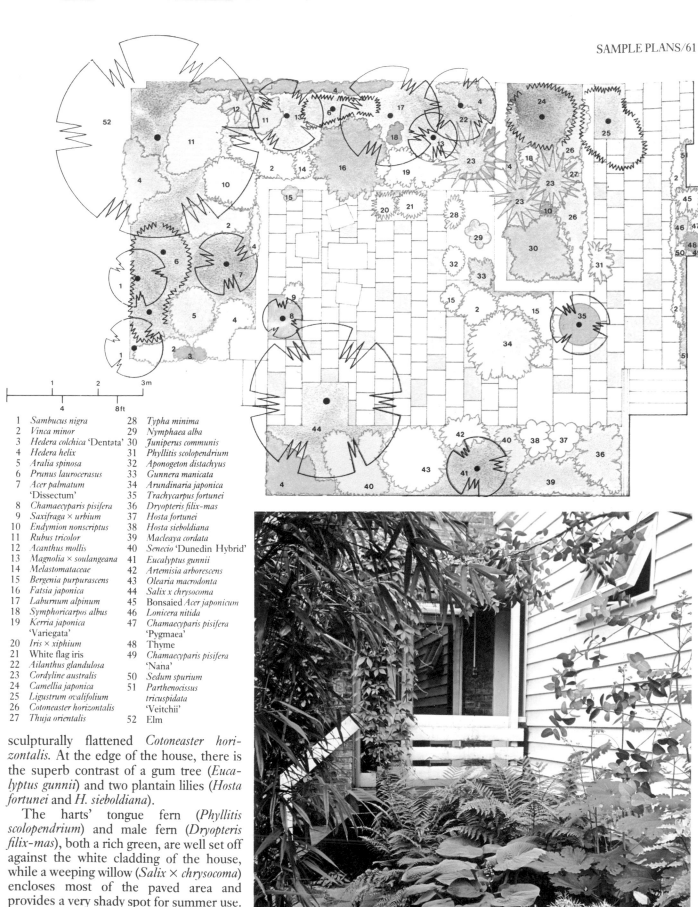

1	*Sambucus nigra*	28	*Typha minima*
2	*Vinca minor*	29	*Nymphaea alba*
3	*Hedera colchica* 'Dentata'	30	*Juniperus communis*
4	*Hedera helix*	31	*Phyllitis scolopendrium*
5	*Aralia spinosa*	32	*Aponogeton distachyus*
6	*Prunus laurocerasus*	33	*Gunnera manicata*
7	*Acer palmatum* 'Dissectum'	34	*Arundinaria japonica*
8	*Chamaecyparis pisifera*	35	*Trachycarpus fortunei*
9	*Saxifraga × urbium*	36	*Dryopteris filix-mas*
10	*Endymion nonscriptus*	37	*Hosta fortunei*
11	*Rubus tricolor*	38	*Hosta sieboldiana*
12	*Acanthus mollis*	39	*Macleaya cordata*
13	*Magnolia × soulangeana*	40	*Senecio* 'Dunedin Hybrid'
14	*Melastomataceae*	41	*Eucalyptus gunnii*
15	*Bergenia purpurascens*	42	*Artemisia arborescens*
16	*Fatsia japonica*	43	*Olearia macrodonta*
17	*Laburnum alpinum*	44	*Salix x chrysocoma*
18	*Symphoricarpos albus*	45	Bonsaied *Acer japonicum*
19	*Kerria japonica* 'Variegata'	46	*Lonicera nitida*
20	*Iris × xiphium*	47	*Chamaecyparis pisifera* 'Pygmaea'
21	White flag iris	48	Thyme
22	*Ailanthus glandulosa*	49	*Chamaecyparis pisifera* 'Nana'
23	*Cordyline australis*	50	*Sedum spurium*
24	*Camellia japonica*	51	*Parthenocissus tricuspidata* 'Veitchii'
25	*Ligustrum ovalifolium*		
26	*Cotoneaster horizontalis*	52	Elm
27	*Thuja orientalis*		

sculpturally flattened *Cotoneaster horizontalis.* At the edge of the house, there is the superb contrast of a gum tree (*Eucalyptus gunnii*) and two plantain lilies (*Hosta fortunei* and *H. sieboldiana*).

The harts' tongue fern (*Phyllitis scolopendrium*) and male fern (*Dryopteris filix-mas*), both a rich green, are well set off against the white cladding of the house, while a weeping willow (*Salix × chrysocoma*) encloses most of the paved area and provides a very shady spot for summer use. The largest plant is an old elm (*Ulmus* spp.) underplanted with periwinkles and ivy.

Despite the range of plants grown in the jungle, this garden requires no more than two half-days a year to maintain its appearance, apart from a regular sweeping-up of leaves in the autumn.

1	Tomatoes	35	Camphor
2	Quince	36	Borage
3	Potatoes	37	Comfrey
4	Sweet corn	38	*Lavandula angustifolia*
5	Cucumber	39	*Lippoia citriodora*
6	Gourds	40	*Aster novi-belgii*
7	Courgettes	41	Beans
8	Marrows	42	Globe artichokes
9	Herbs, including: basil dill, sorrel, cayenne, marjoram, parsley, chamomile, caraway, lovage, fennel, sage, rosemary, thyme, chervil, bay, garlic, juniper, chives, bergamot, winter savory, Russian tarragon, French tarragon, sweet cicely, *Artemisia arbrotanum* and *Artemisia absinthium*	43	Aubergines
		44	*Buddleia crispa*
		45	Loganberries
		46	Gooseberries
		47	Redcurrants
		48	*Vitis vinifera*
		49	*Clematis* × 'Vyvian Pennell'
10	Chicory		
11	*Rhododendron* 'Elizabeth'		
12	*Lonicera japonica*		
13	Mint		
14	*Ficus carica*		
15	Rhubarb		
16	Parsnips		
17	Carrots		
18	*Tropaeolum majus*		
19	*Camellia* × *williamsii*		
20	*Rosa* 'Mme Alfred Carrière' (climber)		
21	*Hedera helix* 'Goldheart'		
22	Lettuces		
23	Peppers		
24	*Fuchsia* 'Brilliant'		
25	*Olearia gunniana*		
26	Sprouts		
27	Strawberries		
28	Radishes		
29	Beetroot	50	Peach
30	Leeks	51	*Ailanthus glandulosa*
31	Broccoli	52	Apricot
32	Horseradish	53	*Wisteria sinensis*
33	Lemon balm	54	*Heliotropium* × *hybridum*
34	Angelica	55	Blackberry

Above *The dainty fronds of a 'tree of heaven' (Ailanthus glandulosa) are well set off by the white-washed wall at one end of this vegetable plot, while a large blackberry has been allowed to ramble across the adjoining section.*

Far right *The uniformity of the raised brick beds has been offset by contrasting foliage and occasional pot plants. Here, the spiky leaves of young globe artichokes grow next to aubergines and outdoor tomatoes and clumps of nasturtiums spill right across the concrete paving.*

The beauty of a kitchen garden

A kitchen garden supplying you and your family with fresh vegetables, fruit and herbs need not be just a rectangular plot with straight rows of plants. It can be designed to be ornamental as well as functional, and still produce just the same amount of crops. A well-designed kitchen garden could rival a flower bed in attractiveness at various times of the year.

The owners of this garden took it over when it had been derelict for some time. The original greenhouse had been vandalized and glass and debris were scattered all over the place. The garden was originally part of a much larger walled garden but, fortunately, the owners had the sunniest south-facing corner.

The first year was spent in clearing a small area of unwanted weeds and removing the broken glass. This area had once been a small herb patch and a few herb plants still survived. To their surprise these herbs started to flourish again and this encouraged the owners to clear up the whole area to grow fruit and vegetables. The old garden walls were whitewashed and the greenhouse repaired and re-glazed. It was decided not to restore the rows of brick-based garden frames but to use the bases for raised vegetable-beds.

The owners were also very fortunate in that a river bordered one side of the garden. Among the rubbish that had been tipped into the river were several old wooden barrels and a park bench. These were rescued and restored for use in the garden.

The plants include a few partly ornamental ones like Chinese asters (*Callistephus sinensis*), nasturtiums (*Tropaeolum majus*) and fuchsias which are grown along the edges of the vegetable-beds and in large flower pots. On the walls, decorative climbers such as ivies, clematis and wisteria provide colour and interest. The grape vine and blackberries provide plenty of edible fruit.

In front of the wall tomatoes thrive, as do fruit trees such as apricots and peaches. Soft fruit which grows well include loganberries, red currants and gooseberries. A 'Brown Turkey' fig (*Ficus carica*), planted in a large barrel to restrict its roots and encourage fruiting, grows in the shelter of the south wall.

The vegetables in the raised bed provide crops at all times of the year. As the garden gets direct sun for most of the day and is

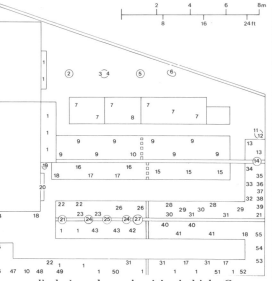

well sheltered, productivity is high. Some of the more exotic vegetables cultivated successfully are courgettes, sweet corn, peppers and aubergines.

Perhaps the most striking thing about this garden is the enormous variety of herbs that are grown – over 30 at the last count. Many of these are characteristically scented, such as camphor, lemon balm, and absinthe, which makes sitting out in this garden such a pleasure.

The overall effect of the garden is predominantly a green haven but the annuals in summer and fruits from late summer onwards provide splashes of colour over a long period.

The garden is built as a series of shallow terraces retained by dark-painted timber walls. The regularity of hedgerows of box and rosemary is softened by colourful groups of pansies, primulas and other annuals.

Terracing a steep site

Very few gardens are on an absolutely flat site, most having a slight slope in one direction or a few hummocks and hollows scattered around the plot. All of these give you great scope to plan your ideal garden. However, there are some sites with such steep slopes that you are quite restricted in what you can do. This garden rises very sharply from the house which is at the very bottom of the slope.

The first priority here was to counteract the feeling that the garden is just about to topple over or slide down into the house. The owners of the site illustrated here decided to overcome this problem by making the main entrance to the garden from the first floor of the house rather than from the ground floor. They built a timber bridge spanning the red-brick, sitting-out area at basement level. From the bridge,

you enter the garden at the second terrace level and go down to the paved area. The terraces stretch across the whole width of the garden making it appear much wider and less steep than it really is. Green-stained timber walls retain the terraces and the width of the garden is emphasized by plantings of clipped box to make horizontal lines of dwarf hedge.

It is basically a fairly rigid layout, as it must be on such an awkward site. No attempt was made to hide the rigidity and in fact this feature has been enhanced by growing sculptural plants such as New Zealand flax (*Phormium tenax*) and African lilies (*Agapanthus* 'Headbourne Hybrids') in bold clumps. To give additional colour several perennials and annuals flower from late spring to early autumn and, nestling in among the various enclosures there are many little corners for sitting or sunbathing.

Bottom *Looking down towards the brick-paved area by the house highlights the enclosed garden atmosphere.*

Below *In this multi-level garden the main emphasis is horizontal, though trees like the flowering cherry in the foreground create interest.*

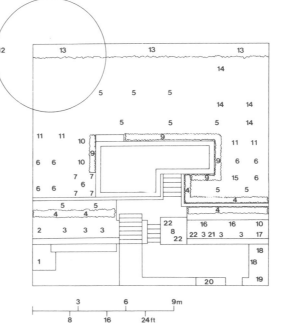

1   *Citrus sinensis*
2   *Phormium tenax*
3   Succulents
4   *Buxus sempervirens*
5   *Fragaria chiloensis*
6   *Raphiolepis* 'Coates Crimson'
7   *Agapanthus campanulatus*
8   *Prunus* 'Shirotae'
9   *Erica × darleyensis*
10 *Viburnum × burkwoodii*
11 *Chaenomeles speciosa*
12 *Quercus ilex*
13 *Ligustrum japonicum*
14 *Arbutus unedo*
15 *Fagus sylvatica purpurea*
16 *Rosmarinus officinalis*
17 *Laurus nobilis*
18 *Primula malacoides*
19 *Betula papyrifera*
20 *Camellia japonica*
21 Parsley
22 *Viola × wittrockiana*

1   *Rosa* 'Dagmar Hastrup'
2   *Rosa eglanteria*
3   *Hosta sieboldiana*
4   Common marjoram
5   Mint
6   Balm
7   Horseradish
8   Burnet
9   Basil
10 Parsley
11 Chives
12 Gooseberry
13 *Rubus trilobus*
14 *Paeonia officinalis*
15 Dill
16 Strawberries
17 *Rubus phoenicolasius*
18 Sweet cicely
19 *Chamaecyparis obtusa* 'Nana Gracilis'
20 *Ilex* 'Veitchii'
21 Summer savory
22 Hyssop
23 Chervil
24 Thyme
25 Sage
26 *Lilium longiflorum*
27 Rhubarb
28 *Petasites japonicus* 'Giganteum'
29 *Lavandula angustifolia*
30 *Buxus sempervirens*
31 *Rosa* 'Peace'
32 *Ruta graveolens*
33 Lovage
34 Sorrel
35 *Asperula odorata*
36 Fennel
37 *Vaccinium corymbosum*
38 *Juniperus squamata* 'Meyeri'

The geometric centrepiece of box hedge.

A pattern of herbs

You probably will not wish to grow only herbs in your garden but, if you have a larger than average plot, a garden-within-a-garden devoted entirely to these plants is very rewarding. The small herb garden shown here is based on a medieval plan with formal herb beds arranged more or less evenly over the site. A few flowers provide colour in the summer months but the herbs provide pleasant scents throughout the year. The two halves of the garden are not exactly the same but they are well balanced.

The garden is entered through an archway cut into an old cypress (*Chamaecyparis obtusa* 'Nana Gracilis') hedge. The central feature is the clipped dwarf box hedge with a solitary rose ('Peace') in the middle. On one side of the garden are two large beds containing dill (*Peucedanum graveolens)* and peonies (*Paeonia officinalis*), and on the other side two narrower, but formal, beds with lavender, lilies, rue (*Ruta graveolens*), rhubarb, and lovage (*Ligusticum scoticum*). Most of the herbs are grown in eight smaller beds offset by a single large rectangular bed planted with blueberry (*Vaccinium corymbosum*), fennel (*Foeniculum vulgare*) and woodruff (*Asperula odorata*).

The circulating and sitting-out area is mainly red-brick paved with gravel in the space around the central box hedge. The western boundary is emphasized by a 16m (50ft) border of the giant butterbur (*Petasites japonicus* 'Giganteum').

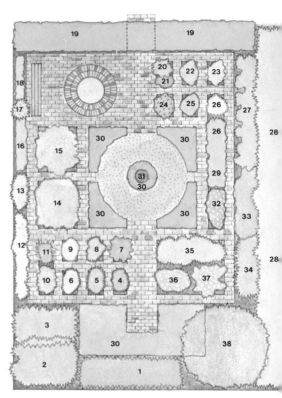

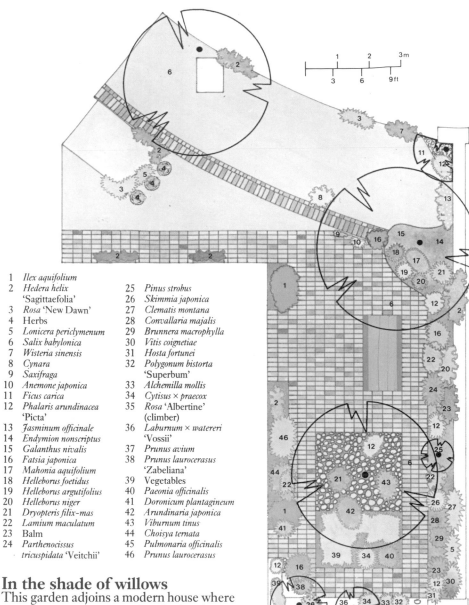

1	Ilex aquifolium	25	Pinus strobus
2	Hedera helix	26	Skimmia japonica
	'Sagittaefolia'	27	Clematis montana
3	Rosa 'New Dawn'	28	Convallaria majalis
4	Herbs	29	Brunnera macrophylla
5	Lonicera periclymenum	30	Vitis coignetiae
6	Salix babylonica	31	Hosta fortunei
7	Wisteria sinensis	32	Polygonum bistorta
8	Cynara		'Superbum'
9	Saxifraga	33	Alchemilla mollis
10	Anemone japonica	34	Cytisus × praecox
11	Ficus carica	35	Rosa 'Albertine'
12	Phalaris arundinacea		(climber)
	'Picta'	36	Laburnum × watereri
13	Jasminum officinale		'Vossii'
14	Endymion nonscriptus	37	Prunus avium
15	Galanthus nivalis	38	Prunus laurocerasus
16	Fatsia japonica		'Zabeliana'
17	Mahonia aquifolium	39	Vegetables
18	Helleborus foetidus	40	Paeonia officinalis
19	Helleborus argutifolius	41	Doronicum plantagineum
20	Helleborus niger	42	Arundinaria japonica
21	Dryopteris filix-mas	43	Viburnum tinus
22	Lamium maculatum	44	Choisya ternata
23	Balm	45	Pulmonaria officinalis
24	Parthenocissus	46	Prunus laurocerasus
	tricuspidata 'Veitchii'		

In the shade of willows

This garden adjoins a modern house where the owners were immediately faced with the common problem of ensuring that the house and garden spaces quickly blended with each other and with the neighbourhood. This was made more difficult than usual when they discovered that one edge of their garden bordered an ancient cemetery. The wall along this side was over 150 years old but their house was newly built. The first thing they did was to plant weeping willows *(Salix babylonica)* to relive the stark angular lines of the house and to give shade to the brick paved area they had laid over the builders' rubble. This particular kind of weeping willow is useful as it is a very vigorous grower and bears its leaves from mid-spring to early winter.

It was soon realized that the fact that there was a burial ground next door could never be competely disguised. It was decided instead to take advantage of its overgrown mystery and use it as a theme for the garden. Mainly shade-loving shrubs have been used, with ground cover over most of the soil surface. To increase the range of plant forms and textures, several ferns and bamboos have also been introduced. The

bulk planting is mainly contrasting greens with the occasional blue or white flowered plants. Climbing on the walls are ivies, clematis and honeysuckles (Lonicera spp.) and there is a minute vegetable plot set in the courtyard.

This garden is not yet complete and it is planned to add a pool with tall reeds and dwarf mosses, as well as some attractive, carefully placed pieces of statuary.

Above *Delicate fronds of weeping willow* (Salix babylonica) *overhang the brick-paved court yard and shelter the bamboos and ferns planted in their shade.*

Right *A small plot in the corner of the courtyard has been planted with vegetables and herbs (cabbage, lettuce and fennel, for example) which are grown as much for their decorative foliage as for eating.*

Top *In this rooftop garden, planting is concentrated along the side walls so that the main weight is distributed at the strongest part of the structure.*

Above *One side has been left unscreened to take advantage of the view over a local park. Wisterias twine up the central supports while among the many container shrubs are* Aucuba japonica, Fatsia japonica *and yuccas.*

Rooftop garden

For some people living in cities, a rooftop may be the only place they have for a garden. The owners of this roof garden live in the adjoining penthouse flat and, over almost 20 years, have created a very successful garden planned as a green and peaceful contrast to the busy streets below.

When they moved in, the flat roof was coverd with asbestos tiles and there were a few built-in planters containing no more than a few pebbles.

The first step was to improve their privacy by screening off the sides, leaving only the narrow side to give them a long south-facing view over the rooftops. Soil was put into the planters and a small pool with a gurgling fountain was made in the space between them. Any water that might overflow is easily led away by the already-installed storm drain.

Climbers such as honeysuckle, wisteria, clematis and the rose 'Albertine' soon covered the bare walls at the back of the planters and, over the years, more climbers have been added so that the stark walls are now almost completely hidden.

Much of the rest of the planting had to be carried out on a trial-and-error basis as some plants did not like the unusual site. Surprisingly, it was often the tender plants that survived and the normally dependable ones that suddenly died. An area like this can be very windy and, in summer, very hot and dry. Plants normally found in Mediterranean regions seem to do particularly well: oleander (*Nerium oleander*) and oranges (*Citrus sinensis*) not only grow in summer but have survived outside in a sheltered spot throughout the coldest

Left *An attractive group of pot plants stands near the apartment wall. They contain white* Alyssum maritimum, *some red pelargoniums, the daisy-like* Anthemis *and several different herbs.*

Below *Small plants in a strawberry pot provide year-round interest: grey foliage of yellow alyssum contrasts the green sea pink (*Armeria maritima*) and* Iberis sempervirens.

months of the winter.

Over the years more large plant containers have been built and planted with a great range of shrubs such as yucca, and the false castor oil plant (*Fatsia japonica*). Pot geraniums (*Pelargonium zonale* and *P. regale*), alyssum and herbs like thyme and mint are grown in small pots grouped together. A white daisy-flowered chamomile (*Anthemis* spp.) has been allowed to establish itself by self-seeding and gives continuity to the many different shapes and sizes of plant pots.

The garden is ideal for sunbathing and out-of-doors eating as it faces south. Lamps have been fixed to the walls so that entertainment can continue into the long summer evenings. In fact, after so many years of effort, this is a very successful garden in a most unusual way.

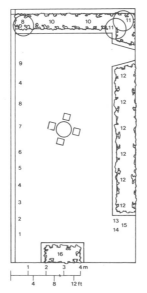

1 *Prunus laurocerasus*
2 *Cotoneaster franchetii*
3 *Helianthemum nummularium* and *Wisteria sinensis*
4 *Aucuba japonica*
5 *Mahonia japonica*
6 *Yucca flaccida*
7 *Armeria maritima*, *Alyssum argenteum*, *Iberis sempervirens* and *Wisteria sinensis*
8 *Fatsia japonica*
9 *Hosta fortunei*
10 Mixed border of *Rosa* 'Halliana' (climber), *Wisteria sinensis*, *Lonicera japonica* 'Halliana', *Agapanthus caulescens* and *Senecio* 'Dunedin Hybrid'
11 *Hydrangea macrophylla*
12 Mixed border of *Clematis montana*, *Lonicera japonica halliana*, *Forsythia ovata*, *Hedera*, various roses
13 *Nerium oleander*
14 *Laurus nobilis*
15 *Citrus sinensis*
16 *Pelargonium*, *Alyssum maritimum* and herbs

1 *Chamaecyparis lawsoniana*
   'Ellwoodii'
2 *Cotoneaster*
   melanocarpus laxiflorus
3 *Dianthus deltoides*
4 *Aubrieta deltoidea*
5 *Lavatera olbia*
6 *Gypsophila paniculata*
7 *Iris germanica* 'Joanna'
8 *Phlox subulata*
9 *Geranium psilostemon*
10 *Juniperus communis*
   'Hornibrookii'
11 *Gentiana lagodechiana*
12 *Salvia turkestanica*
13 *Typha latifolia*
14 *Bergenia* 'Silberlicht'
15 *Anemone vitifolia*
16 *Helianthemum nummularium*
17 *Campanula portenschlagiana*
18 *Festuca glauca*
19 *Sedum spectabile*
20 *Centranthus ruber*
21 *Stokesia laevis* 'Blue Star'
22 *Rosa* 'Baroness Rothschild'
23 *Physostegia virginiana*
24 *Yucca flaccida*
25 *Saponaria ocymoides*
26 *Delphinium*
27 *Chelone obliqua*
28 *Buddleia farreri*
29 *Epimedium pinnatum*
30 *Iberis sempervirens*
31 *Geranium pratense*
   'Johnson's Blue'
32 *Spiraea japonica* 'Alpina'
33 *Echinops banaticus*
34 *Taxus baccata*
35 *Vaccinium corymbosum*
36 *Mahonia pinnata*
37 *Picea abies* 'Echiniformis'
38 *Rosa* 'White Wings'
39 *Bergenia* × 'Morgenröte'
40 *Aconitum arendsii*
41 *Alchemilla mollis*
42 *Primula pulverulenta*
43 *Astilbe* × *arendsii* 'Red
   Sentinel'
44 *Tradescantia virginiana*
45 *Iris laevigata* 'Monstrosa'
46 *Hemerocallis* 'Black Prince'

47 *Primula florindae*
48 *Pennisetum compressum*
49 *Cornus kousa chinensis*
50 *Jeffersonia diphylla*
51 *Aruncus dioicus*
52 *Rhododendron forrestii repens*
53 *Nymphaea indiana*
54 *Iris kaempferi*
55 *Hemerocallis* 'Bonanza'
56 *Astilbe* × *arendsii*

'Professor van der Wielen'
57 *Rodgersia pinnata*
58 *Primula rosea*
59 *Hosta sieboldiana* 'Elegans'
60 *Betula pendula* 'Youngii'
61 *Lysichiton camtschatcense*
62 *Astilbe* × *arendsii* 'Fanal'
63 *Astilbe* × *arendsii* 'Erica'
64 *Petasites japonicus* 'Giganteum'
65 *Petasites hybridus*

4   8m

12   24ft

A water garden

This garden is dominated by the high enclosing cypress hedges and by the pools. However, there is still plenty of room for land plants as well as a wide variety of aquatic specimens. The main area of water is L-shaped but there is also a smaller pool separated from the long edge of the 'L' by a narrow path. The straight edges of the pools are softened in places by bold plantings of the giant reedmace (*Typha latifolia*) and a vigorous water-lily *Nymphaea indiana* in the water, and grasses such as *Pennisetum compressum* on the pool edge.

A series of long flower beds stretching almost the whole length of the site are planted with a range of flowering shrubs and herbaceous plants stepped-up against the background hedge. The idea behind the major planting is contrasting plant forms and leaf textures and shapes. However, there is plenty of summer colour from plants such as *Geranium* 'Johnsons Blue', wall valerian (*Centranthus ruber*) and the rock roses (*Helianthemum nummularia* and its many varieties).

Sitting out is possible anywhere on the stone-paved area but a favourite spot is under the large yew tree opposite the main flower beds.

The overall effect of the garden is one of contrasting areas linked together by a sense of completeness and by the pools. Despite the formal appearance of the plan, however, the garden is also both rambling and full of interest – a difficult blend to achieve.

Right *Dense foliage in the main pool stands out against the long flower bed behind. Plants include the giant reedmace,* Typha latifolia, *with a clump of* Pennisetum compressum *to the right and water lilies to the left.*

A heather garden

Acid sandy soils are not generally as fertile as clay or chalky soils, and the choice of plants that will thrive tends to be limited. However, nearly all the very attractive heathers (*Erica* spp.) prefer an acid soil, so a heather garden is an obvious choice for these conditions. This particular plot was awkward because it sloped steeply away from the house towards the drive and access road.

It was planned in a way that would get rid of the difficult slopes by making a series of low terraces retained by dwarf walls cut into the slope. These were built as dry-stone walls so that water would not collect behind them and waterlog the soil. The curved pattern of the levels was emphasized by hedges of dark-green yews contrasting greatly with the paler and blue-green leaved heathers. In addition, some of the yellow-leaved and red-leaved heathers were grown.

Heathers are available with a good range of flower colours from purest white to deep pinks, and many of these varieties have been planted in this garden.

As well as the heathers, other acid-loving and acid-tolerant species have been included in this design. Rhododendrons, brooms and dwarf conifers are planted along the edges to give height. Bulbs are used to grow through the heathers for colour when the heathers are still dormant.

As an added bonus, this garden is virtually weed-free and requires little maintenance.

Below *Mixed planting of heathers has created soft mounds of rich colour on the front terraces. Variation in the height and foliage comes from the broom (Genista lydia)* in the foreground and Juniperus chinensis *in the middle. The pampas grass at the back is planted in the neighbouring garden; there is no formal boundary, so that the adjoining lawns run together.*

1	*Pyracantha coccinea*	14	*Rosa* 'Evelyn Fison'
2	*Rosa* 'Anna Wheatcroft'	15	*Potentilla fruticosa*
3	*Chamaecyparis lawsoniana* 'Stewartii'	16	*Cytisus scoparius*
4	*Rhododendron japonicum*	17	*Viburnum carlesii*
5	*Erica cinerea* 'Lavender Lady'	18	*Cytisus scoparius*
6	*Erica carnea* 'King George'	19	*Hebe* 'Pagei'
7	*Erica carnea* 'Springwood White'	20	*Rhododendron fastigiatum*
8	*Erica cinerea* 'Rosea'	21	*Fritillaria imperialis*
9	*Calluna vulgaris* 'Gold Haze'	22	*Erica x darleyensis*
10	*Erica cinerea* 'C.D.Eason'	23	*Rhododendron* 'Blue Diamond'
11	*Calluna vulgaris* 'Alilportii'	24	*Rhododendron* 'Praecox'
12	*Juniperus sabina* 'Tamariscifolia'	25	*Hebe* 'Autumn Glory'
13	*Calluna vulgaris* 'H. E. Beale'	26	*Cytisus praecox*
		27	*Cotinus coggygria*
		28	*Iris germanica*
		29	*Senecio* 'Dunedin Hybrids'
		30	*Rhododendron* 'Vanessa'
		31	*Betula papyrifera*
32	*Crataegus oxyacanthoides*		
33	*Polyanthus*		
34	*Prunus cerasifera* 'Nigra'		
35	*Cotoneaster horizontalis*		
36	*Rhus typhina*		
37	*Pinus mugo pumilio*		
38	*Taxus baccata* 'Fastigiata'		
39	*Genista hispanica*		
40	*Geranium subcaulescens*		
41	*Calluna vulgaris* 'Mrs Ronald Gray'		
42	*Juniperus × media* 'Pfitzerana Aurea'		
43	*Calluna vulgaris* 'Alba Plena'		
44	*Iris pumila*		
45	*Genista lydia*		
46	*Chamaecyparis pisifera*		
47	*Chamaecyparis lawsoniana* 'Fletcheri'		
48	*Lithospermum diffusum* 'Grace Ward'		
49	*Calluna vulgaris* 'Foxii Nana'		
50	*Rhododendron impeditum*		
51	*Chamaecyparis obtusa*		
52	*Daphne collina*		
53	*Rhododendron* 'Elizabeth'		
54	*Chamaecyparis lawsoniana* 'Columnaris'		
55	*Dryas octopetala*		
56	*Picea glauca*		
57	*Saponaria ocymoides*		
58	*Lonicera nitida*		
59	*Skimmia japonica*		
60	*Primula juliae* 'Wanda'		
61	*Corylopsis pauciflora*		

INDEX

Picture Credits

Front cover: Michael Warren

A-Z Collection: 21(tc); Molly Adams/landscape architect Nelva Webber: 34(bl); Elly Arnstein/Tony Timmington: 21(cr); Walter Bauer: 25(r); Steve Bicknell: 1.11(t), 21(bl), 22, 23(t,c,b), 24(l), 32/33, 34(tr), 34(br), 35(t), 37, 49(l,r), 66, 67, 68, 68/9, 69, 70; R. J. Corbin: 52(b); Crowsons: 52(t); Douglas Dickens: 29; Valerie Finnis: 42, 43(t); Susan Griggs Agency: 47 Michael Boys, 49(br); Nelson Hargreaves: 28; Hovel: 30(tl,br); P. Hunt: 40/1; George Hyde: 27; I.M.S.: 24(r); Harold King: 54(t); Bill McLaughlin: 8(l), 21(br), 60, 61; Elsa Megson: 11(b); Paul Miles: 21(tr,cl,c), 33(t); Han Njio: 39; Murial Orans Horticultural Photography: 32; The Picture Library/Nick Holt: 35(b); Picturepoint: 5; Roger Phillips: 13, 19; R. Procter: 45(tl); Richardsons: 53(r); J. Roberts: 9(t); Ianthe Ruthven: 62, 63; Ruth Rutter: 48(r), 53(l); Kim Sayer: 9(b); Harry Smith Horticultural Photographic Collection: 25(l), 33(b), 40(t,b), 42/3, 43(b), 45(bl), 48(l), 51; Wolfram Stehling: 30(r); Peter Stiles: 21(tl); Syndication International: 75; G. S. Thomas: 10; Transworld: 64, 65; Michael Warren: 15, 20, 21(bc), 28/9, 34(tl), 45(tr,br), 54(b), 58/9, 59; Colin Watmough: 7; Elizabeth Whiting: 8(r) Jerry Tubby, 54/5; Michael Wickham: 2/3; Joyce Wreford: 50.